THE STORY OF BRITISH COLUMBIA

Far West

The Story of British Columbia

Daniel Francis

Harbour Publishing

Harbour Publishing Co. Ltd.
P.O. Box 219, Madeira Park, BC, V0N 2H0
www.harbourpublishing.com

Cover painting *Perez in* Santiago *off Langara Island, 1774* by Gordon Miller
Cover, text and map design by Roger Handling, Terra Firma Digital Arts
Illustrations by Drew Kennickell
Edited by Mary Schendlinger

Additional photo credits: Page 1: Logging with horse team, Vancouver Public Library Special Collections S-6546; pages 2–3: First Train between Montreal and Coast, Norman Denley Collection, Library and Archives Canada PA-066579; page 6: *Mailboat – CPR Wharf, Vancouver 1887*, Gordon Miller; page 7: Front Street, New Westminster, 1904, Vancouver Public Library Special Collections 6749; pages 38, 153, 154, 163, 164–165, 169, istockphoto.

Printed in China

Harbour Publishing acknowledges financial support from the Government of Canada through the Book Publishing Industry Development Program and the Canada Council for the Arts, and from the Province of British Columbia through the BC Arts Council and the Book Publishing Tax credit.

THE CANADA COUNCIL | LE CONSEIL DES ARTS
FOR THE ARTS | DU CANADA
SINCE 1957 | DEPUIS 1957

BRITISH
COLUMBIA
ARTS COUNCIL
Supported by the Province of British Columbia

Library and Archives Canada Cataloguing in Publication

Francis, Daniel
    Far west : the story of British Columbia / Daniel Francis.

Includes index.
ISBN 13:978-1-55017-410-6
ISBN 10:1-55017-410-X

    1. British Columbia—History—Juvenile literature. I. Title.

FC3811.2.F73 2006   j971.1
C2006-903338-2

To my grandson Riley

CONTENTS

Two generations of coastal vessels. The Senator (l.) was a wooden vessel built in 1880 to ferry passengers and mail back and forth across Burrard Inlet, the future site of Vancouver. Behind it, the Cutch was the first vessel owned by the Union Steamship Company when it began operations on the BC coast in 1890. *Gordon Miller painting*

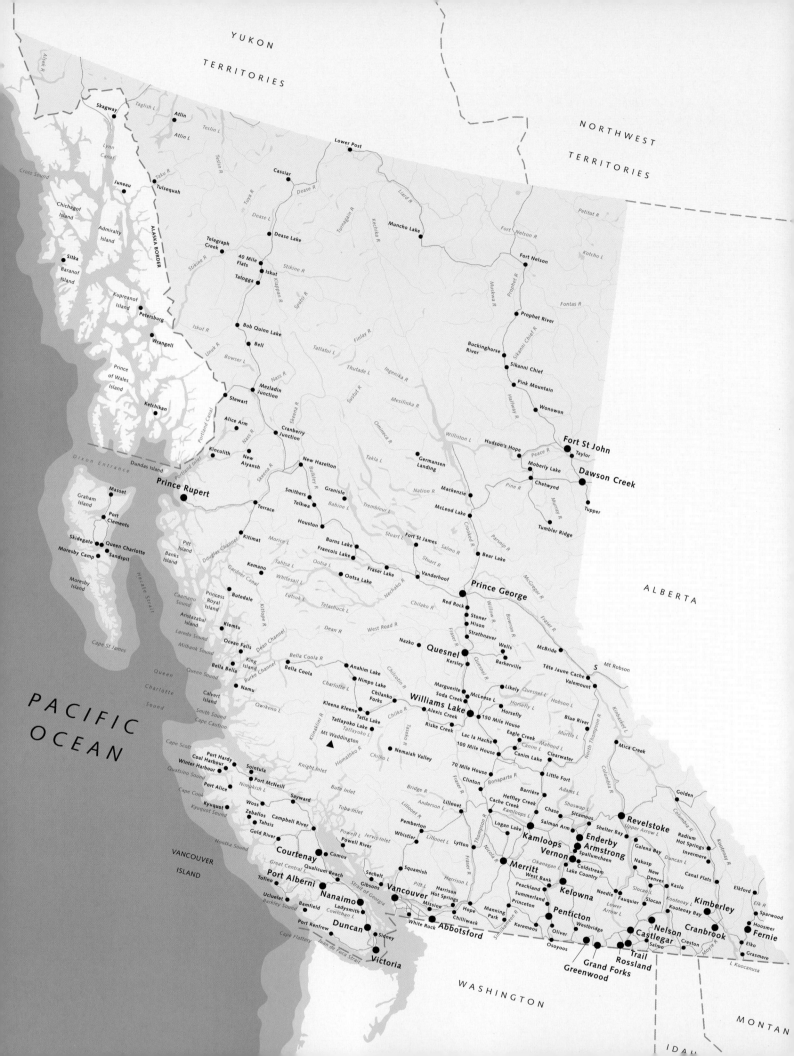

New settlers bringing in the hay on their farm in Chilliwack. Chilliwack Museum and Archives P227

INTRODUCTION

Compared to other places, the province we call British Columbia is not very old. The land has been around forever, and the First Nations and their ancestors have lived here for thousands of years. But the rest of us are recent arrivals. British Columbia was one of the last places to be visited by the European navigators who explored so much of the globe. The province itself was created less than two hundred years ago—a blink of an eye in the history of the world.

Still, a lot has happened in British Columbia. People have come here from all over the world in search of wealth and a new way of life. First Nations people have created rich cultures going back many generations. Together British Columbians have used the resources of this place and their own knowledge and ingenuity to make a unique society.

Far West is the story of that society. It introduces you to the history of the place and to many of the people who played a role in getting things done. You will meet the First Nations people and learn about their cultures. You will meet some of the explorers and fur traders who were the first outsiders to venture into the land. You will meet the gold seekers and the railway builders, the loggers and the coal miners, the politicians and the artists. And that is just the beginning!

An awful lot has happened in British Columbia, and all of it has been interesting.

This dramatic painting shows one of the ocean-going canoes made by the Nuu-chah-nulth people of Nootka Sound on Vancouver Island. *Gordon Miller painting*

THE ORIGINAL PEOPLE 1

Gordon Miller painting

Aboriginal people have lived in British Columbia for thousands of years. They were hunters and fishers who relied on the land and its many resources to provide everything they needed for their survival.

About 250 years ago the first Europeans arrived in British Columbia. They thought that they had "discovered" the territory because no other explorers had been there before them. But British Columbia was already occupied by many

This giant canoe, Red Raven, made by Bill Reid is 15 metres long and held more than a dozen paddlers. Canoes like this one were used by the Haida (HY-dah) people, who lived on the Queen Charlotte Islands, also known as Haida Gwaii (HY-dah-GWY). Canadian Museum of Civilization

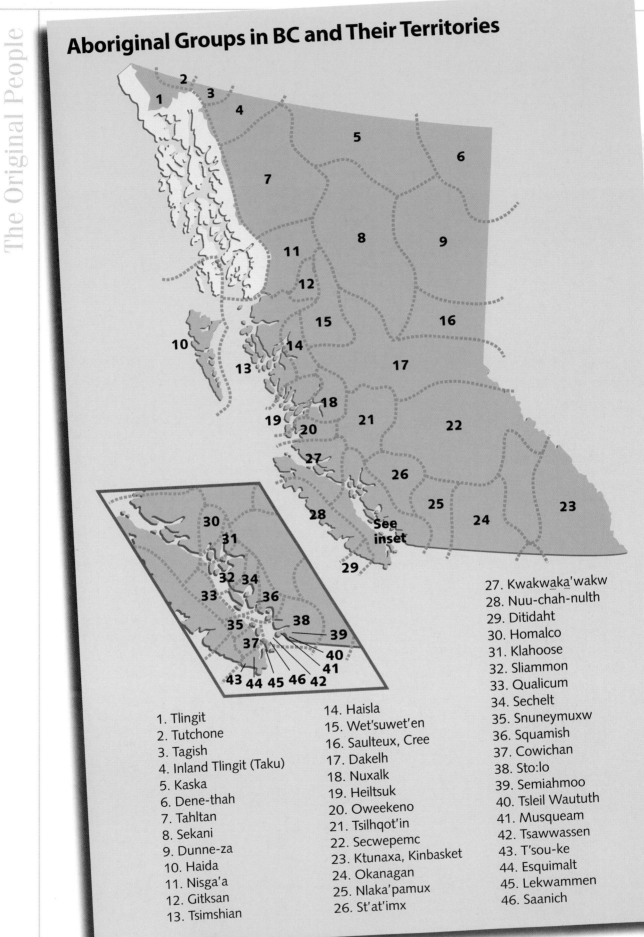

Aboriginal Groups in BC and Their Territories

1. Tlingit
2. Tutchone
3. Tagish
4. Inland Tlingit (Taku)
5. Kaska
6. Dene-thah
7. Tahltan
8. Sekani
9. Dunne-za
10. Haida
11. Nisga'a
12. Gitksan
13. Tsimshian
14. Haisla
15. Wet'suwet'en
16. Saulteux, Cree
17. Dakelh
18. Nuxalk
19. Heiltsuk
20. Oweekeno
21. Tsilhqot'in
22. Secwepemc
23. Ktunaxa, Kinbasket
24. Okanagan
25. Nlaka'pamux
26. St'at'imx
27. Kwakwaka'wakw
28. Nuu-chah-nulth
29. Ditidaht
30. Homalco
31. Klahoose
32. Sliammon
33. Qualicum
34. Sechelt
35. Snuneymuxw
36. Squamish
37. Cowichan
38. Sto:lo
39. Semiahmoo
40. Tsleil Waututh
41. Musqueam
42. Tsawwassen
43. T'sou-ke
44. Esquimalt
45. Lekwammen
46. Saanich

different groups of people when the explorers arrived. They were the Aboriginal people, the ancient ancestors of the First Nations people who live in British Columbia today.

These original people did not need to be discovered. They had been living in their territories for as long as anyone could remember.

Digging Up the Past

Archaeologists have found evidence that people were living in British Columbia at least 10,500 years ago. This evidence consists of stone tools and spear points found buried in the ground at ancient hunting camps. The people who made these objects were big game hunters. They tracked down giant bison, moose, caribou and mountain sheep, and killed them with stone spears. They ate the meat and used the skins to make tents and clothing. They were the long-ago ancestors of today's Aboriginal people.

As time passed, the number of people living in British Columbia grew. They inhabited the valleys of the Interior and the islands and inlets along the coast. Slowly they developed different languages and different ways of life. Over the years they evolved into the many Aboriginal groups that were present in British Columbia when the first explorers arrived.

People of the Coast

The Aboriginal groups living along the seacoast followed a way of life that was different in many ways from that of groups living in the Interior. On the coast the climate is mild and wet. Warm air blows in off the ocean, and as it rises to cross the mountains it drops its load of moisture as rain. The BC coast is one of the wettest spots on earth. The moisture nourishes lush forests of cedar, spruce and hemlock trees. The coastal rain forest, as this area is known, contains some of the tallest trees in the world.

The land and climate had a strong influence on the coastal people's way of life. The rain forest provided them with everything they needed. They built large houses made from planks cut from the trees. They used the trunks of the trees to make their canoes, and the bark and roots to weave clothing, mats, fish nets, rope and baskets. Today, Aboriginal people still use wood to carve the totem poles and masks that are such an important part of their culture.

On the coast, people lived by fishing, collecting shellfish and hunting seals and sea lions. Some even hunted giant whales in the ocean far from shore. Every spring a silvery fish called the eulachon (*OO-lah-kun*) swarms in huge numbers at the mouths of the rivers. These fish are very greasy. They provided fuel to burn for light, as well as oil to spread on food.

Spearheads in the collection of the Royal British Columbia Museum. BC Archives Image 1514

A modern artist, Gordon Miller, used old photographs to make this painting of a Haida village as it looked 150 years ago. The Haida are a coastal people. The village, called Ninstints, is gone now, though some of the totem poles remain. *Gordon Miller painting*

When they dried, the eulachon burned just like candles. The coastal people traded eulachon oil to other groups living in the Interior for furs, meat and hard obsidian glass, which they used to make tools.

The people of the coast were sea-going people. Some of them lived on islands. Their villages were always at the water's edge. They had no roads or wheeled vehicles. They travelled everywhere by water in their log canoes. These canoes were beautifully shaped, polished and decorated with designs and carvings. They were works of art, made by trained artisans.

During the winter the people lived in large villages of many houses. It was during the winter, when the weather was bad, that they socialized and carried on their dances and religious ceremonies. When better weather came in the spring, they moved to smaller camps to fish, hunt seals and gather shellfish. Sometimes these camps were built atop middens, which are piles of discarded clam and oyster shells many metres deep. Archaeologists dig into the middens and discover evidence that people have used them for thousands of years.

People of the Interior

In the Interior of British Columbia, Aboriginal groups lived a different kind of life. Here the climate was drier. It was much colder in the winter and hotter in the summer. The people lived in small groups of one or two families. They moved around a lot, pursuing deer, moose and caribou, which were their main foods.

Salmon was another important food for people in the Interior. Salmon are born in the freshwater streams of the Interior, then follow the rivers out to the ocean. There they stay until their life is nearly over. Then they return to fresh water to spawn near the same spot where they were born. As the salmon made their way up the rivers toward the Interior, Aboriginal people all along the way caught them in nets or

BC Creatures
PACIFIC SALMON

There are five types of Pacific salmon (top to bottom): sockeye, pink, chum, chinook and coho. Each type is slightly different in appearance and has different life habits. Fisheries and Oceans Canada

speared them at the rapids. The people of the Interior dried the salmon in the sun, or smoked them over open fires to preserve them so that they would have delicious meals of salmon all through the winter months.

During fishing season, the Interior people gathered together in central villages. Here they harvested the fish, met with their relatives,

Two First Nations fishers make repairs to their salmon trap, called a weir. When the trap was submerged in the water, the salmon swam into it and could not find a way out again. BC Archives G-03/43

feasted and carried on important ceremonies. When the fishing was over, the people went away in smaller groups to hunt animals and to gather berries and roots.

Nuu-chah-nulth Whalers

The Nuu-chah-nulth are a coastal people. For as long as anyone can remember, they have lived on the west coast of Vancouver Island. Like other coastal people, the Nuu-chah-nulth made their living from the sea. They fished for salmon and herring, hunted seals and sea lions, and gathered clams and oysters from the rocky shore. The meat and oil from these animals was stored for use during the winter months.

The Nuu-chah-nulth had a special skill. They were the only people on the coast who hunted whales. These giant animals swim past the coast of British Columbia on their way to and from their summer feeding grounds in Alaska.

A young Nuu-chah-nulth (new-CHAH-nulth) girl at Alberni on Vancouver Island in 1910. Alberni Valley Museum, 3160

BC Spotlight
ABORIGINAL HOUSING

Aboriginal people on the coast lived in large dwellings known as longhouses, or big houses (A). They were made of planks cut from cedar trees. Several families that were related to each other lived in each house. The outside of the house was decorated with paintings, and large, carved poles stood at the entrance.

In the Interior, people lived in lodges made from animal skins, or sometimes in pit houses (B). To make a pit house, they dug a shallow hole in the ground. Then they built a frame of poles over the hole and covered it with animal skins or dirt. They went in and out of the house through a hole in the roof and a ladder. This cozy shelter kept the people warm in the winter. Each village contained many pit houses.

Other people lived in shed houses (C). These were plank houses as well, but their roofs were flat and sloped from the front to the back. Sometimes the houses stood alone; sometimes they were joined end-to-end in a long line.

Standing on the beach, the Nuu-chah-nulth could see the whales splashing and blowing in the waves offshore.

The whale hunt required great courage and skill. Whalers enjoyed a special place in Nuu-chah-nulth society. They were usually chiefs who had spent years preparing themselves for the hunt. They learned the animal's habits and went through many rituals to try to influence the way it behaved. They bathed themselves in cold water, went for long periods without food and sang special songs. They had to prove that they were worthy of matching themselves against the whale.

When they were ready, the members of a whaling crew climbed into their huge cedar canoe and set out into the open ocean. It was dangerous work. They would be on the water many days. A storm might blow up and overturn the canoe, or winds might carry them far from shore.

Once the whale was sighted, paddlers had to sneak up on it when it surfaced to take a breath.

GIANTS OF THE SEA

There are many different kinds of whales in the ocean. The Nuu-chah-nulth hunted the gray whale, one of the largest species. Gray whales come from Mexico, where they spend the winter in large warm-water lagoons, and the females give birth and nurse their young. Early in the year the whales leave Mexico and swim up the coast of North America all the way to Alaska. It is a trip of about 9,500 kilometres. No other mammal travels as far in a single year.

After spending the summer near Alaska getting fat on the tiny animals that live in the water there, the whales return to the south. On their way to and from Alaska, the whales pass the territory of the Nuu-chah-nulth.

hurry. A wounded whale reacted with a violent slap of its tail, then dove below the surface to escape. If the canoe was too close, it could easily be swamped or smashed to pieces.

The chase was on. The harpoon was attached to the canoe by a long line. The fleeing whale pulled the hunters along behind it. They could do little but wait for the wounded animal to grow tired. When it came up for air, other harpoons were planted. Gradually the whale weakened from loss of blood until finally it died.

By this time the hunters might be far out to sea. They lashed the dead whale to the canoe and began the long paddle back to their village. The journey might take many days of hard labour. When finally they reached the beach, the whale was butchered and shared among all the people in the village. There was feasting and singing to

When they were almost on top of it, the chief thrust his long harpoon deep into the whale's back. Then the paddlers had to back away in a

BC Places

WHALERS' WASHING HOUSE

This whaling shrine was located near the village of Yuquot (YOU-kwaht) on Vancouver Island. It was called the Whalers' Washing House. It contained many carved figures of humans and whales. Hunters stopped here and washed themselves with purifying water before the hunt. In 1904 these particular items were sold to a museum in New York City, where they remain today. A group of Nuu-chah-nulth are trying to have them returned to their village.

Canadian Museum of Civilization, 20512

This painting by Emily Carr, completed in about 1912, is called House Front—Gold Harbour. *It shows one of the cedar plank houses built by the First Nations people.* Vancouver Art Gallery

Gray whales are still being chased by humans. Today, though, the "hunters" are tourists armed with cameras who merely want to watch the majestic animals as they swim past. Jacqueline Windh photo

thank the spirits for allowing the whale to be taken. The Nuu-chah-nulth believed that if they failed to perform these rituals, they would be unsuccessful the next time they went hunting.

A single whale supplied tons of meat and oil for food, and bone to make tools and utensils. It was a way for hunters to show their skill and gain prestige in the village. All Nuu-chah-nulth respected a successful whaler.

Every year the hunters killed a few whales. One animal could feed a whole village, so there was no reason to kill very many.

Then, beginning in the 1850s, American whalers began killing the gray whales in great numbers. So many of them died that for a while it was believed that the gray whale was extinct. The Nuu-chah-nulth had to give up whaling because there were no whales to hunt.

The killing stopped in time to save the whales from extinction, however. They survived and began to grow in numbers until today there are as many gray whales as there ever were. The Nuu-chah-nulth are even talking about hunting them again. Meanwhile, the whales have become a tourist attraction. Large numbers of visitors to Nuu-chah-nulth territory travel in boats off the coast to see the whales in their natural habitat.

Making Contact

The Haida were the first Aboriginal group in BC to meet with Europeans. This happened in 1774, when the *Santiago*, a Spanish sailing ship 25 metres long, arrived near one of the Queen Charlotte Islands on a voyage of exploration. Nine Haida paddlers came out from shore in a canoe to have a look at the strangers, then more canoes came out. The Haida brought food and

This painting imagines the meeting in 1774 between the Spanish vessel Santiago *and the Haida near the Queen Charlotte Islands. It is believed to have been the first time any local First Nations had met with Europeans.* Gordon Miller painting

furs to trade, but before the Spanish could land, a wind blew the *Santiago* away from the coast.

Four years later, in 1778, more ships appeared on the coast, this time in the territory of the Nuu-chah-nulth people. Captain James Cook was exploring the Pacific coast for the King of England. He brought his two ships, *Discovery* and *Resolution*, to Vancouver Island in search of a safe harbour and fresh water for his sailors.

When two people who were as different as the Nuu-chah-nulth and the explorers meet, they often do not understand each other. They are seeing so much for the first time. The

Captain James Cook with his two vessels, Resolution and Discovery, arrives at Resolution Cove in Nootka Sound in 1778. Cook stayed at the cove for almost four weeks, repairing his ships, collecting water and wood, and learning about the local people, the Nuu-chah-nulth, who had made him welcome. Gordon Miller painting

The Original People

In Their Own Words

JAMES KING

James King, a sailor with Captain Cook, described what he saw when the Europeans approached shore in Nootka Sound:

The first men that came would not approach the ships and seemed to eye us with astonishment, till the second boat came that had two men in it. The figure and actions of one of these men were truly frightful. He worked himself into the highest frenzy, uttering something between a howl and a song, holding a rattle in each hand. From time to time he took handfuls of red ochre and bird feathers and spread them in the sea. This was followed by a violent way of talking.

—Adapted from *The West Coast (Nootka) People* by Eugene Arima (BC Provincial Museum, 1983), pp. 119–20.

Below is a painting by John Weber, another member of Cook's crew. It shows the sailors trading at the village of Yuquot, or Friendly Cove, where the Nuu-chah-nulth people lived.

Nuu-chah-nulth had never seen sailing ships. They thought that the tall-masted vessels were floating houses. Captain Cook and his men did not understand the language of the Nuu-chah-nulth or the ceremonies they used to welcome visitors to their territory.

The Nuu-chah-nulth people used to be known as the Nootka. This name came from a misunderstanding on the part of Captain Cook and his crew. The story goes that Cook motioned in the air with his finger and asked what the area round about was called. The people thought he was asking for sailing directions. They told him to sail around the island, using a word that sounded like *nootka*. Cook thought they were telling him that they were the Nootka. That is what he called them, and so they were called that for many years. Only recently have the people begun to use their own name, Nuu-chah-nulth.

Potlatch dancers arriving at a coastal village for a feast.
Gordon Miller painting

BC Places

NAMING PLACES

Aboriginal people often take their names from physical features. The word *Nuu-chah-nulth*, which means "all along the mountains," refers to the territory where the Nuu-chah-nulth people live, below the mountains on the coast of Vancouver Island.

Ucluelet (*you-CLEW-let*) is an important Nuu-chah-nulth village. Its name means "wind blowing into the bay." The village near where the people met Captain Cook became known as Friendly Cove. Its actual name is Yuquot, meaning "where the wind blows from all directions." Wickaninnish, one of the beaches on the coast, is named after a local chief. Its name means "no one in front of him in the canoe," which shows that he was the most important person in the community.

The Potlatch

For many Aboriginal groups in British Columbia, the potlatch was the most important ceremony. The word *potlatch* comes from the Nuu-chah-nulth word *patshatl*, meaning "giving." It refers to the fact that gift giving is an important part of the potlatch. So are dancing, songs, feasts and storytelling.

The potlatch is at the heart of the Aboriginal way of life. A potlatch is held at important times in the life of individuals and the community. Some potlatches are held to celebrate weddings, or to mourn the dead. Others celebrate the raising of a totem pole, or the naming of a new chief.

In the old days, potlatches took a long time to

prepare and lasted for several weeks. Nowadays they usually last for a day or two. Guests receive presents from the host before they return home.

Aboriginal people relied on the world around them to provide all their needs. This woman was a member of the Nlaka'pamux (Ing-khla-KAP-muh) people, who live along the Fraser River. All her clothing is made from animal skins, even her hat, which is decorated with bird feathers. *Canadian Museum of Civilization 23212*

The presents are a token of thanks to the guests for attending the potlatch and witnessing the important ceremonies that took place.

When Europeans arrived in British Columbia, they did not understand the potlatch. They saw the Aboriginal people gathering together to give away their possessions and they thought it was wasteful and evil. They wanted the people to give up their old ways and become more like Europeans. In 1885, the government outlawed the potlatch. Anyone taking part in the ceremonies was sent to jail.

The ban on the potlatch lasted for sixty-five years. It was a great blow to Aboriginal culture. The ceremonies that were such an important part of their life could not be held. The people were known for their masks and headdresses carved out of wood. Most of these carvings were made for the potlatch ceremonies. Since the potlatch was forbidden, the arts of the Aboriginal people went into decline.

The law did not stop the potlatch altogether. The people continued to hold a few ceremonies in secret, but they had to break the law to do so. Finally the government decided that the law was unjust. In 1951, the potlatch again became legal. Today it continues to be an important ceremony among Aboriginal people, and once again the arts of the people are flourishing.

Totem poles are still being made by Aboriginal carvers. They are a familiar sight in British Columbia.
Jacqueline Windh photo

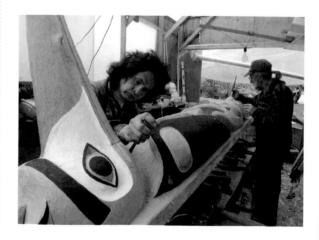

Totem Poles

One of the most familiar parts of Aboriginal culture in British Columbia is the totem pole, a tall pillar of carved wood. Skilled carvers made each pole from a single cedar log.

Totem poles depict figures from Aboriginal history and legend, and important crests and designs from the owner's family. Anyone who understands what the designs mean can read a pole like a book.

There were different kinds of poles. Some stood on the beach in front of the village to

(Left and above) As well as totem poles, carvers made wooden masks that dancers wore during ceremonies. The masks might represent real animals or creatures from myth and legend, or they might transform from one to the other with moving parts. BC Archives D-08362 and E-04017

welcome visitors. Others stood in front of a house to show the family history. Still others stood in the graveyard to honour dead relations. All of these poles had great significance for the people.

Young carvers learn their skills by studying as apprentices with older carvers. They learn techniques handed down through many generations. In this way the Aboriginal people keep their traditions strong.

Storytellers

Long ago the Aboriginal people had no system of writing. Instead, they recorded their history and passed on their traditions in stories, songs and dances. Rather than reading books, an Aboriginal person learned by listening to the elders, watching the ceremonies and studying the objects made by artists.

Many Aboriginal artworks and stories are about animals. The people believe that the way to learn about life is to study nature and learn from it. The lessons of nature are expressed in the art and ceremonies of the people.

The Original People

Bill Reid was an artist who belonged to the Haida people who live on the Queen Charlotte Islands. He made many beautiful sculptures. This one is called "The Raven and the First Men." It shows the first people emerging from a clamshell, as told in one of the Haida creation stories. The sculpture is on display at the Museum of Anthropology at the University of British Columbia. Collection of the UBC Museum of Anthropology, Vancouver, Canada. Bill McLennan photo

Elders are very important people in Aboriginal society. They are respected advisors who use their knowledge and experience to guide younger people. Elders keep alive the traditions of the group.

A New Beginning

The arrival of Europeans brought great changes to the Aboriginal world. The newcomers brought many things that were of value to Aboriginal people. Metal kettles, knives, guns and blankets were useful items that were quickly adopted by the people. In return, they traded furs and food and shared their knowledge of what Europeans called the New World.

For many years, life for the Aboriginal people went on much as before. The newcomers came from time to time in their ships, or set up small forts in the Interior. The Aboriginal people traded with them from time to time, but their way of life did not change a great deal.

More and more outsiders arrived in British Columbia, however. They spread disease, used up the resources and threatened to take away the land. This presented a new challenge to the Aboriginal people. They had welcomed the newcomers into their land. Now they were learning to live with the consequences.

History Mystery

THE VOYAGE OF FRANCIS DRAKE

In the summer of 1579, an English sailing captain named Francis Drake arrived in the Pacific Ocean in his ship, the *Golden Hind*. Drake was a pirate who made his living by raiding other ships belonging to the Spanish and stealing their cargo. He was also an explorer, and the Queen of England asked him to become the first English navigator to sail around the world.

Drake's voyage was a great secret because the Queen did not want anyone to know her plans. As a result, no one knows even today exactly where he went. We do know that he attacked many Spanish towns and ships in South America. Then he sailed north up the coast, past what is now California. Some say he reached Vancouver Island. Others think he got all the way to the Queen Charlotte Islands. Others say he did not reach British Columbia at all. Either way, it was two hundred years before Europeans again visited this part of the coast.

Drake arrived back in England with the hold of his ship crammed with plunder. Queen Elizabeth made him a knight and he bought a great castle for himself. But Drake never stayed on dry land for long. He took part in many more naval battles against the Spanish. During one of these expeditions, he died of yellow fever.

This painting shows Captain James Cook in his vessel
Resolution *entering Nootka Sound in 1778.*
Gordon Miller painting

THE ARRIVAL OF THE TRADERS

Fort Langley Historic Park, Mike Starr photo

Traders from many countries were attracted to British Columbia. They came in search of sea otter and beaver skins, which the Aboriginal people offered in trade. The fur trade brought many changes for the Aboriginal people.

In 1778, when Captain James Cook arrived near the village of Yuquot on what is today Vancouver Island, some of his men traded with the Nuu-chah-nulth people who lived there. The sailors offered knives, blankets and metal tools. In return, they received food and furs.

Ships from Great Britain and the United States came to the coast to trade manufactured goods for furs. It was the first meeting of Aboriginal people and Europeans in British Columbia.

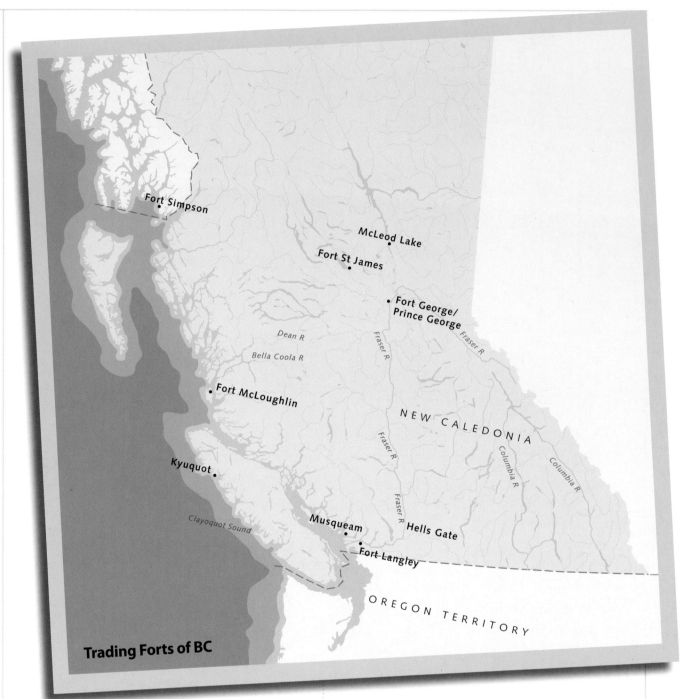

Trading Forts of BC

After leaving the coast of British Columbia, Cook sailed his ships back across the Pacific Ocean to China. At the famous market city of Canton, his men sold the furs at a great profit. Chinese merchants were most impressed with the quality of the sea-otter pelts. Thick and soft, they made the finest fur coats.

Before long, word spread to other trading nations about the valuable furs. The result was a rush of ships to the coast of British Columbia.

In Search of a Passage

While the trade in furs flourished, exploration of the coast continued. The Spanish, who already owned what is now Mexico to the south, hoped to expand into the north. The Russians were planning expeditions from their posts in Alaska. And the British, thanks to Captain Cook's visit, thought that they had a claim on the area.

Into this confusing situation sailed Captain George Vancouver. He was one of the leading

This is Captain Vancouver's cabin aboard his ship, the Discovery. *It has been rebuilt at the Royal British Columbia Museum in Victoria.* Royal British Columbia Museum

explorers in Great Britain. He came with orders to survey the coastline of North America between California and Alaska, and to enforce Britain's claim to ownership.

Between 1792 and 1794, Vancouver and his men spent three summers on the coast. They anchored their ship, the *Discovery*, offshore and used smaller rowboats to look into every cove and inlet. The sailors sweated at the oars under the hot sun or through the driving rain. At night they camped in tents on the hard, rocky shore. It was exhausting work, but when they were finished, they had drawn the first accurate map of the British Columbia shoreline.

Meanwhile, the Russians withdrew from the coast, leaving the British and the Spanish to come to an agreement. Eventually the Spanish agreed to give up their claim. The two nations signed a treaty. Anyone could trade on the coast, but the area now belonged to Great Britain.

Of course, no one asked the Aboriginal people. As far as they were concerned, the land belonged to them. After all, it had belonged to their ancestors for thousands of years. This different view of things continues right down to the present.

The Sea Otter Trade

The traders came mainly from Great Britain and the United States. Each summer they sailed their small ships along the coast. When they came near a village, they sounded a cannon to announce their arrival. The local Aboriginal people came out in canoes, bringing with them their furs to trade. When all the goods had been exchanged, the ship moved on to the next village. Before the autumn storms arrived, traders sailed across the Pacific to China, where they bartered their furs for tea, silk and spices. These goods were much in demand in Europe.

The Aboriginal people were smart traders. They were used to trading among themselves and knew how to drive a hard bargain. They knew the goods they wanted, and how to haggle for the best price. At the height of the trade, vessels swarmed all over the coast. If one trader would not offer a fair price, the people could always wait for another vessel to come along.

The trade for sea-otter pelts only lasted a few years. The demand was so high that thousands were slaughtered every year. By about 1820, so many sea otters had been killed that they were becoming hard to find. Sea-going traders were replaced by permanent trading posts that specialized in land-based furs such as beaver. The focus of the fur trade shifted from the coastal villages to the rivers and lakes of the Interior.

Crossing the Continent

At the same time as the sea-otter traders were cruising the coastal waters in their ships, other traders were trying to find a route to the Pacific by land. For many years they had been trading with the Aboriginal people of the Plains and the eastern woodlands (what are now the Prairie provinces and eastern Canada). The Rocky Mountains, however, presented an impassable barrier that kept the traders out of the Interior of British Columbia.

FAST FACT

During the mid-1790s, traders collected 20,000 otter pelts a year on the coast. By 1830, they traded for fewer than 400 pelts.

BC Creatures
THE SEA OTTER

The sea otter is a sleek, speedy animal related to the weasel. It spends most of its time in the water and feeds by diving to the ocean floor to gather sea urchins and shellfish. The sea otter is one of the few animals that uses tools. When it finds a shellfish, it cracks it open with a stone to get at the meat inside.

Sea otters grow thick coats of fur to keep themselves warm. In the trading days, this fur was worth ten times as much as a beaver pelt. It was so valuable that traders called it "soft gold."

The trade in furs killed off almost all the sea otters on the Pacific coast. In 1911 an international treaty banned the hunt, but it was too late. Along the British Columbia coast, the animal disappeared. Then, during the 1960s, sea otters from Alaska were moved to British Columbia. Today there are several hundred of them living in BC waters.

BC People
FRANCES BARKLEY

The first European woman to visit British Columbia was Frances Barkley. When she was seventeen years old, she married Charles William Barkley, a sea captain, in England. Together the newlyweds set sail on a trading voyage in a ship called *Imperial Eagle*.

It was a honeymoon unlike any other. First of all the ship almost sank in a raging storm. Then Captain Barkley came down with a fever and almost died. Finally, in June 1787, the *Imperial Eagle* reached Yuquot, where the crew traded for furs.

A few weeks later the Barkleys sailed south into a huge bay, which they called "Wickaninnish's Sound" after the powerful chief who lived there. Today it is called Clayoquot (*CLAY-oh-kwaht*) Sound. Farther south the Barkleys visited another large inlet filled with beautiful islands. Today it is Barkley Sound, a favourite spot for whale watching and kayaking.

The Barkleys had many more adventures on the high seas before they returned to their home in England.

The fur trade in the rest of Canada was dominated by two large companies. The Hudson's Bay Company, owned by British merchants, traded from the shores of Hudson Bay. The North West Company was based in Montreal. Both companies operated a network of trading posts across the continent, and both companies wanted to discover a route across the mountains to the Pacific.

The North West Company sent Alexander Mackenzie, one of their most experienced traders, to find a route to the ocean. With the help of Aboriginal guides, Mackenzie made his way on foot through the snowbound mountain passes. He came down out of the mountains to a great river, now called the Fraser. He and his men and Aboriginal guides set off by canoe to see where the river would take them.

Grease Trails

The Aboriginal people knew British Columbia well. For many centuries they had followed a network of footpaths that led from the coast to the Interior. Along these trails they carried food and other items for trade between the different tribes. One of the most important trade items was oil from the eulachon, a coastal fish. Aboriginal people from the coast carried

Alexander Mackenzie, the first person to cross North America. BC Archives PDP02244

the oil to the Interior, where it was much in demand as a food delicacy and as fuel for lighting. That is why the trails they followed became known as "Grease Trails."

It was down one of the Grease Trails that the Aboriginal guides led Alexander Mackenzie all

Lady Washington *was one of the ships belonging to the American sea-otter traders. It is shown trading at Ninstints, a village in the Queen Charlotte Islands, in 1791.* Gordon Miller painting

the way to the Pacific. On July 22, 1793, they reached the mouth of the Bella Coola River where it empties into the Pacific. This made Mackenzie the first European to cross North America from the East.

River to the Sea

Other traders followed Mackenzie into the western mountains. In 1805 they established the first trading post west of the Rocky Mountains, at a place called McLeod Lake.

One of the traders, Simon Fraser, led another expedition in search of a route to the Pacific. The route that Mackenzie had followed was too difficult. Fraser hoped to find an easier passage.

In 1808, Fraser and his men set off by canoe down the river that now bears his name. Once again they relied on Aboriginal guides to show them the way. It was a terrifying trip through steep canyons and over swirling rapids. Fraser stopped at several villages along the way. At one

BC Places
MACKENZIE ROCK

Mackenzie paddled to a rock and used a mixture of grease and dye to write:

Alexander Mackenzie, from Canada, by land, the twenty-second of July, one thousand seven hundred and ninety-three.

Visitors to this place at Elcho Harbour in Dean Channel can still read the message scrawled on the rock. Today it is preserved as a historic site.

BC Archives A-02312

of these, a place called Kumsheen, the people were so excited to see him that he had to shake hands with every person in the village.

When the rapids became too dangerous, Simon Fraser and his companions had to creep along the walls of the canyon. They used wooden scaffolds built by their Aboriginal guides. They clung to the rock by their fingertips while the water swirled below them.

At last Fraser and his group reached the mouth of the river, near a place called Musqueam (*MUS-kwee-um*), which today is part of Vancouver. But once again the river had proved to be too dangerous for regular use by fur-trade canoes. Another trader later said, "I consider the passage down the river to be certain death, in nine attempts out of ten."

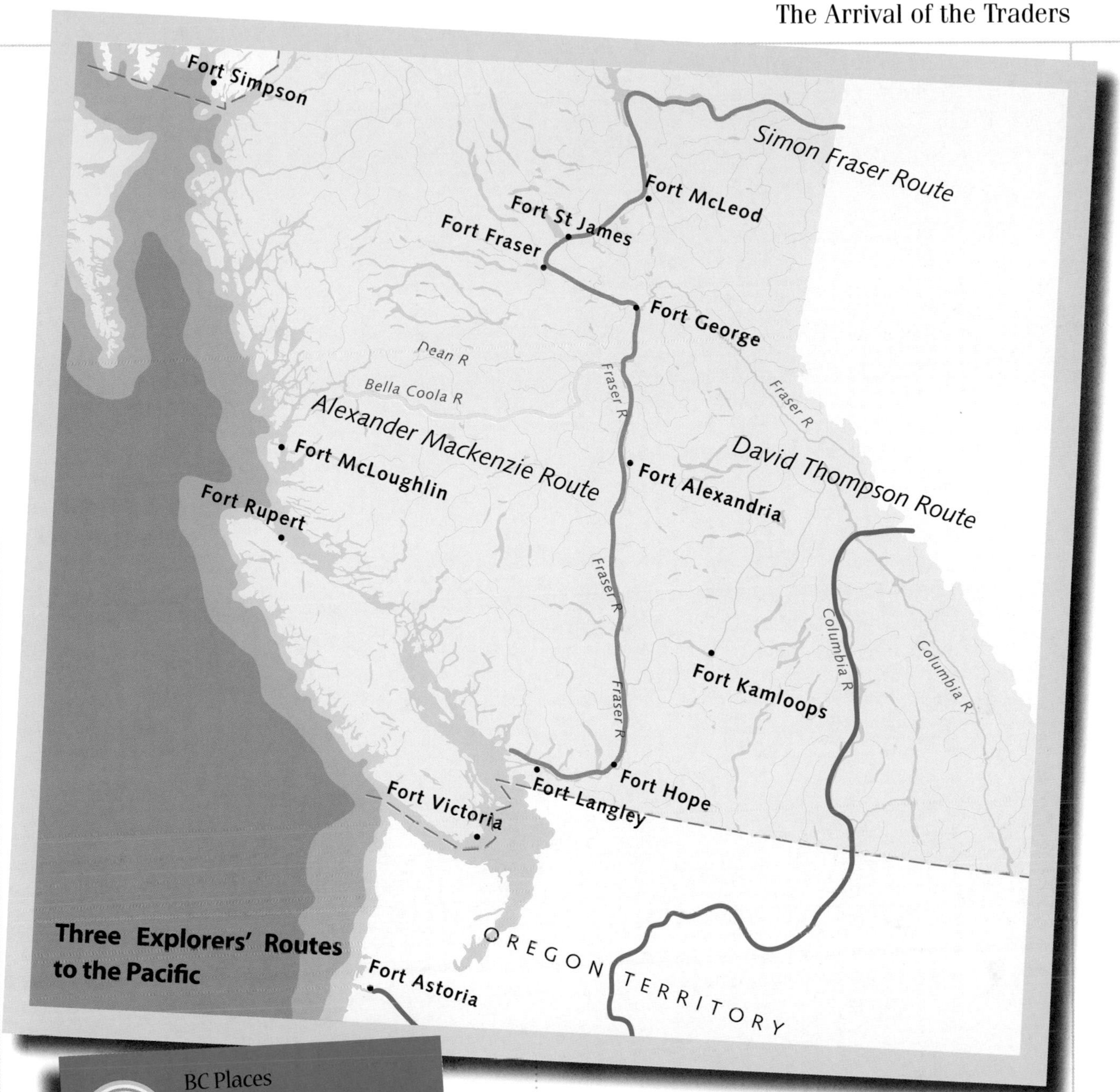

Fort Simpson

Simon Fraser Route

Fort McLeod

Fort St James

Fort Fraser

Fort George

Dean R

Bella Coola R

Alexander Mackenzie Route

Fort McLoughlin

Fraser R

David Thompson Route

Fort Rupert

Fort Alexandria

Fraser R

Columbia R

Columbia R

Fort Kamloops

Fort Hope

Fort Victoria

Fort Langley

Three Explorers' Routes to the Pacific

O R E G O N   T E R R I T O R Y

Fort Astoria

BC Places
HELLS GATE
The narrowest point on the Fraser River is a place called Hells Gate. When the water is high in the spring, it rips through this gorge at over 30 kilometres an hour.

This map shows the three routes used by explorers to reach the Pacific from the Interior.

Fur Trade in New Caledonia

When Simon Fraser arrived in northern British Columbia, he called the area New Caledonia. The lakes and hills of the Interior reminded him of his mother's stories of her home in Scotland, also known as Caledonia. Other traders called this area "the Siberia of the fur trade" because it was so far from home and so cold in the winter.

Fraser and his men were Nor'westers. They belonged to the North West Company, one of

The riddle of the rivers was finally solved by a third explorer, David Thompson. In 1811 he travelled down the Columbia River to the ocean. Unlike the other rivers, the Columbia turned out to be safe and convenient. Traders began using it as the main corridor connecting the Interior with the coast.

The Arrival of the Traders

the two giant trading companies that controlled the trade. In New Caledonia the Nor'westers had a monopoly. For many years their rivals from the Hudson's Bay Company did not follow them across the mountains.

It was difficult and expensive to import food to feed the traders at their isolated posts. They grew a few vegetables, but for the most part they relied for their survival on the Aboriginal people who brought fish, deer meat, berries and other food.

Aboriginal hunters also supplied the furs on which the trade was based. Mostly the traders wanted beaver furs, which were used to make fancy hats in Europe. But they also took muskrat, marten, fox and bearskins. During the winter the Aboriginal people travelled to their hunting grounds in small family groups. In the spring they brought their furs to the post, where they traded for tools, guns, blankets and cloth.

Every summer the voyageurs loaded their canoes with the furs they had traded and began their long trip east. They crossed the Rocky Mountains through one of the high passes and descended to one of the company's trading posts in Alberta. There they dropped off the furs and picked up more trade items to take back with them to New Caledonia. It was the fur trade that first tied British Columbia to the rest of Canada.

BC Places
TRADING POSTS
The Nor'westers built a string of trading posts across the interior of New Caledonia. One of these posts was Fort George, now the modern city of Prince George. Another, Fort St. James, is a historic site where some of the original building still stands.

Fort Langley as it looks today. Mike Starr photo

A FUR-TRADE FORT: Fort Langley National Historic Park

Fort Langley was a typical fur-trade post. As its name suggests, it was built like a small fort. A wall of logs surrounded an inner courtyard where there were rooms for the men, a dining hall, a warehouse, repair shops and a store where trading took place.

Surrounding the fort were fields where the company grew potatoes, grain and other things to eat. The land around Fort Langley turned out to be so fertile that the post was soon growing produce for other posts in the territory. It took a lot of hard work to plant seeds, keep the fields free of weeds, and harvest the crop when it was ready. For this work the company hired Aboriginal people from nearby villages. Today this area of British Columbia, in the valley of the Fraser River, is still the centre of farming in the province.

At Fort Langley the traders also obtained salmon from the Aboriginal people. They salted it to keep it from spoiling, then packed it in barrels for shipment to Hawaii, where it was sold.

Over the years the buildings at Fort Langley fell into disrepair. Then, during the 1950s, to celebrate British Columbia's 100th birthday, some of the post was rebuilt. Today it is a historic site that people can visit to learn more about life in the early fur trade days.

FAST FACT

Most of the men who worked for the North West Company were French-Canadian voyageurs. Or they were Métis (MAY-tee), a mix of French and Aboriginal. For this reason the working language of the fur trade in British Columbia at this time was French.

When the wind was strong, the Beaver was powered by sails in order to save fuel. When the wind died, it started up its engine. *Gordon Miller painting*

The Hudson's Bay Company

In 1821 the Hudson's Bay Company absorbed its longtime rival, the North West Company, and took over all the Nor'west posts in New Caledonia. From 1821 the fur trade belonged solely to the Bay Company.

One of the changes made by the HBC was to set up trading posts closer to the coast. The first of these was Fort Langley, built on the Fraser River in 1827. It was followed by Fort Simpson and Fort McLoughlin in the north.

For years the headquarters of HBC trade was at Fort Vancouver on the Columbia River, in what was called the Oregon Territory. Furs reached the fort from New Caledonia down a well-used route. Traders from all the Interior posts brought in their furs by canoe to Fort Alexandria. There they were loaded on packhorses and carried overland along a trail to Fort Kamloops and down through the Okanagan Valley to the upper Columbia River. At this point the furs were put on boats that descended the river to Fort Vancouver, where they were loaded onto ships. Trade goods imported from Europe followed the same route, only in the opposite direction.

The Beaver *was a work boat on the coast for 50 years. It met its end when it was wrecked one day near the entrance to Vancouver harbour. The remains of the vessel still lie in deep water underneath the Lions Gate Bridge linking Vancouver to West Vancouver.*
BC Archives A-00009

Great Britain and the HBC hoped to keep control of the Oregon Territory, but in the 1840s American settlers began moving in from the eastern United States. The US government served notice that it wanted Oregon for itself. For a while it looked as though Britain and the Americans might go to war over the land. Finally, after years of negotiation, they reached a compromise. The Oregon Territory became part of the United States and the border with British territory was set at its present position along the 49th parallel of latitude.

The new border left the HBC with a bit of a problem. Its headquarters, Fort Vancouver, was now in American territory. The company decided to move north to Vancouver Island where it built a new post, Fort Victoria, overlooking a fine harbour. This small settlement became the headquarters of all the fur trade in British Columbia and it later became the provincial capital, Victoria.

The Hudson's Bay Company supplied the posts along the coast with trade goods and food by sailing ship. In 1836, there was great excitement at the posts when the company brought a new supply vessel out from England. Called *Beaver*, it was the first steam-powered ship on the Pacific coast. It was a sign that the Age of Sail was giving way to the Age of Steam.

A Fur-Trade Language

When fur traders arrived on the coast, they found many different Aboriginal groups speaking many different languages. The traders themselves spoke either French or English. In order for everyone to understand one another, people came up with a new language. It was called Chinook jargon.

Chinook jargon was mix of words—some English, some French, some Aboriginal, some entirely new. Anyone wanting to do business on the coast had to learn it. At one time Chinook

BC Spotlight
CHINOOK JARGON
Words from the Chinook jargon dictionary:
tyee: chief
tillikum: friend
klahowyah: greetings, or hello
cheechako: newcomer, or stranger
skookum: strong, brave
saltchuck: ocean
These are just a few of more than seven hundred words in this unique language.

jargon was spoken by a quarter of a million people. It died out with the end of the fur trade, and now only a few people know it.

Aboriginal People and the Fur Trade

Traders and Aboriginal people were partners in the fur business. Each needed the other. Traders supplied the Aboriginal people with goods they could not get elsewhere. Guns, kettles, blankets and needles were just some of the items the Aboriginal people came to value.

For their part, the Aboriginal people supplied the traders with valuable furs. As well, they guided the outsiders on their trips into the wilderness, and they provided food to the posts. The traders would not have been able to survive without the help of the Aboriginal people.

The fur trade did not lead to settlement by newcomers. It required only a few posts scattered around the territory. The Aboriginal people did not have to fear that the traders would take their land.

Still, the fur trade did bring important changes for Aboriginal people. They came to rely on goods from the outside world, and this gave the traders power over them. As well, the people and goods coming and going through trade carried diseases that were common in Europe but unknown in North America. The

Aboriginal people had no immunity to measles, smallpox, tuberculosis or whooping cough, and they died in great numbers.

The worst epidemic occurred in 1862. In March, a sailor infected with smallpox arrived in Fort Victoria aboard a sailing ship from California. The infection spread to the Aboriginal people who were camped around the outskirts of the fort. When they returned to their villages up the coast, they carried the disease with them. By summer, smallpox was passing up the rivers into the Interior. For two years the epidemic raged. When it was over, about one-third of all the Aboriginal people in British Columbia, as many as 20,000 people, had died.

The spread of disease was the worst result of the contact between Europeans and Aboriginal people.

Creating a Colony

Even though the border between Oregon and British territory was established in 1846, the British feared that Americans might move north and claim even more territory. They decided the best way to prevent this was to send out British settlers to live on Vancouver Island.

> **FAST FACT**
> According to the law at the time, a person needed to own at least 8 hectares of land to be allowed to vote. Only 43 colonists qualified.

In 1849 the British declared the island to be a British colony. The Hudson's Bay Company was granted control of all the trade in the area. In return, the British government asked the company to bring out settlers and pay the costs of getting them established as farmers. For the time being, the mainland was left to the Aboriginal people and the few traders who lived there.

Government of the colony was in the hands of Governor James Douglas and a few officials. The British insisted that a government should be elected, and in 1856 the first elections were held. Seven people were elected, and on August 12, 1856, the first elected government in what would become British Columbia held its first meeting.

Colonists on Vancouver Island grew crops to feed themselves and workers at the fur-trade

---

BC People

THE KANAKAS

The Hawaiian Islands are located in the middle of the Pacific Ocean, about halfway between North America and the Orient. Ships carrying furs and other goods from the Pacific coast to China stopped at these islands to take on supplies and do some trading. In those days they were called the Sandwich Islands.

The Native people of the islands were good sailors. Some of them signed on as crew members of the trading ships. In this way they ended up in British Columbia, where they were known as Kanakas. (*Kanaka* is a word from the Pacific islands meaning "human being.")

Hawaiians helped to build Fort Langley and Fort Victoria. It was not unusual to find one or two working at any of the trading posts in New Caledonia. Most were men. Some of them married Aboriginal women and settled down to live in British Columbia permanently.

Many people living in British Columbia today can trace their ancestry back to the original settlers from Hawaii.

BC People
A GOVERNOR AND HIS LADY

Amelia Connolly was a daughter of the fur trade. Her father, William Connolly, was the trader in charge of Fort St. James in New Caledonia. Her mother was a Cree woman from the Prairies. Amelia Connolly had lived at many trading posts across western Canada.

In 1828, when she was sixteen years old, she married James Douglas, a clerk at the fort. They moved to Fort Vancouver, where Douglas rose through the ranks to become the most important Hudson's Bay Company official on the coast. He founded Fort Victoria, and when Vancouver Island became a colony, he became the governor.

Amelia Douglas was now "First Lady" of the colony. She preferred the simple life of a fur-trade post, but she learned to carry out the official duties of a governor's wife.

BC Archives A-01227

BC Archives A-01234

posts. In the north of the island, coal mines produced coal that was sold to the British navy and to Americans in San Francisco. There was also some logging and sawmilling. Otherwise, Vancouver Island was a fur-trade outpost at the far edge of the world. One person described it as "a kind of England attached to the continent of North America." Not many settlers wanted to come to live in such an isolated spot. The island was left to the Hudson's Bay Company to rule pretty much as its own private fiefdom.

GOLD RUSH! 3

In 1858, prospectors arrived in British Columbia to look for gold. The rush of gold seekers lasted for several years. It led to the growth of business, the construction of roads and towns, and the creation of the first government on the mainland.

From Furs to Gold

The fur trade attracted very few settlers to British Columbia. Traders were interested only in collecting furs, not in starting farms or building towns. Besides, the Interior of British Columbia was a sea of mountains. There seemed to be little good land for growing crops.

It was gold that brought the first flood of newcomers to British Columbia. During the 1850s, First Nations people began finding nuggets in the gravel banks of rivers flowing through the Interior, and took them to trade. In California, where rich finds of gold had been discovered, prospectors had already been busy for several years. The California treasure trove was playing out, however, and gold seekers were looking elsewhere for new finds. When word leaked out that there was gold in the rivers of British Columbia, it touched off a stampede of miners.

New Arrivals

The first group of gold seekers arrived at Fort Victoria by ship from San Francisco in March 1858. These men hit the jackpot when they found a rich deposit of gold in the Fraser River gravel at a place called Hill's Bar, not far from Yale. When people found out, the rush was on. As many as thirty thousand newcomers arrived in Victoria within just a few months. Most

FAST FACT
Only about 500 settlers and traders lived in Victoria before 30,000 prospectors and business people arrived.

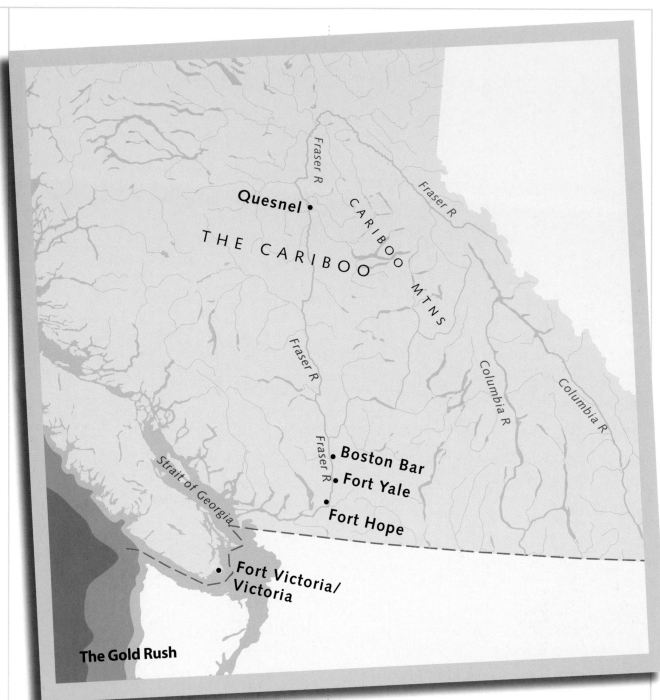

Quesnel •

THE CARIBOO

C A R I B O O   M T N S

Fraser R

Fraser R

Fraser R

Columbia R

Columbia R

Fraser R

• Boston Bar

• Fort Yale

• Fort Hope

Strait of Georgia

• Fort Victoria/
Victoria

The Gold Rush

were prospectors who immediately headed for the mainland. Others were business people who hoped to make a profit selling supplies. They purchased land and built stores and warehouses. Tiny Fort Victoria blossomed into an instant city. "Innumerable tents covered the ground as far as the eye could see," reported one observer, the Reverend Matthew Macfie. "The sound of hammer and axe was heard in every direction."

Prospectors heading for the goldfields had to cross the Strait of Georgia to the mainland using whatever means possible—paddlewheel steamboat, canoe, rowboat or homemade raft. Some people drowned in the headlong rush to be first to the gold.

Once they reached the mouth of the river, they travelled upstream about 150 kilometres to the Fraser Canyon above Fort Hope, where the water narrowed into a deep gorge. This was where the first gold was found, on the gravel banks and sand bars like Hill's Bar. Camps sprang up beside the river with names like Boston Bar, China Bar, Texas Bar and many others. The sleepy village of Yale became headquarters for

the rush, where prospectors bought supplies, banked their gold and celebrated in the bars and saloons. Gamblers and thieves were as plentiful as miners, and the typical Yale resident slept

A paddlewheeler has arrived at the busy riverfront town of Yale in 1866. The steamboats were so shallow that they could land simply by running into shore. Vancouver Public Library Special Collections 23430

Gold Rush!

with a gun under the pillow. In the opinion of one reporter, "a worse set of cut-throats and scoundrels never assembled anywhere."

The First Nations people who lived in the area were taken aback by the sudden flood of American gold seekers into their land. The Fraser River between its mouth and Fort Yale was the territory of the Sto:lo people. Farther up the river beyond Yale was the territory of the Nlaka'pamux (*Ing-khla-KAP-muh*), "the people of the canyon." Both groups relied on the plentiful runs of salmon in the river for their livelihood. They were dismayed by the crowd of outsiders, who disrupted the fishery and overran their camps. The First Nations also came to believe that they should receive something in return for the gold that was being taken from their territory. They blocked the river and drove the prospectors from their diggings. It was war, and lives were lost on both sides before peace was made.

But nothing could stop the miners, who moved like a rising tide north up the river, seeking gold in all the streams and valleys nearby. Most of all they were looking for the motherlode, the big vein of gold that was the source of all the grains and nuggets they had been collecting from the river. They travelled on the trails shown to them by the First Nations. Eventually they arrived at the Cariboo Mountains east of Quesnel (*kweh-NELL*),

BC People
MIFFLIN GIBBS

A few Black people joined the gold rush to British Columbia. They were tired of being treated as second-class citizens in the United States, where slavery was legal. Among them was Mifflin Gibbs, a merchant from California. He settled in Victoria and opened a general store. In 1866 he won election to the city council, and later he served as acting mayor. When the American Civil War ended slavery in the US, Gibbs returned with his family to live there.

BC Provincial Archives B-01601

where they made several of the biggest strikes. By the 1860s the Cariboo was the centre of the gold rush.

In the Cariboo, mining was done differently

In Their Own Words
THE LITTLE CAPITAL

An early visitor, George Grant, described what Victoria was like in the early days:

A walk through the streets of Victoria showed the little capital to be a small polyglot copy of the world. Its population is less that 5000; but almost every nationality is represented. Greek fishermen, Jewish and Scottish merchants, Chinese washermen, French, German and Yankee officeholders and butchers, negro waiters and sweeps, Australian farmers and other varieties of the race, rub against each other, apparently in the most friendly way. The sign boards tell their own tale. "Won Shing, washing and ironing"; Sam Hang, ditto; "Kwong Tai & Co., cigar store"; "Magazin Francais"; "Teutonic Hall, lager beer"; "Scotch House"; "Adelphic" and "San Francisco" saloons; "Oriental" and "New England" restaurants....

From *Ocean to Ocean*, George Monro Grant (Prospero Books, 2000).

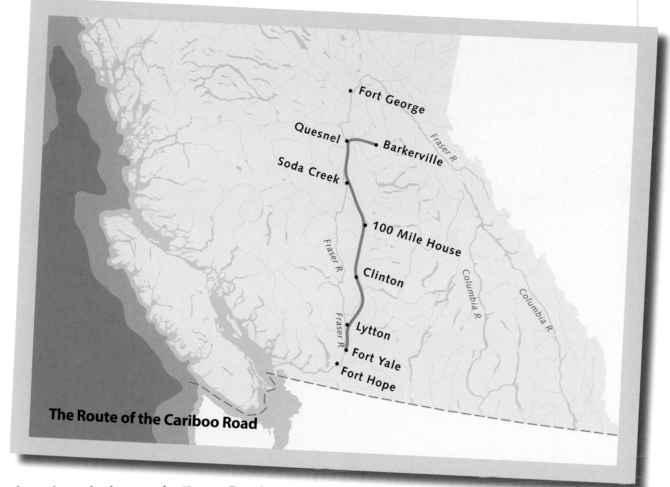

The Route of the Cariboo Road

from the early days on the Fraser. Panning no longer produced most of the gold. Instead the miners began digging into the ground in search of the veins of precious ore that ran through the rock. They had to sink deep shafts and buy heavy equipment. All of this cost a lot of money, well beyond the means of a lone prospector with not much more than a packsack of food and a pickaxe. Gradually large companies bought up the mines, and prospectors became paid employees who laboured for a wage.

Building the Cariboo Road

The Cariboo was a long way from the coast. Steamboats could take people up the Fraser River as far as Yale, but after that it was untracked wilderness. There were no roads, and the paths used by First Nations people were steep and dangerous. Pack horses fell and broke their legs. The woods were full of bears, and the mosquitoes and blackflies drove

prospectors crazy. The cost of carrying supplies to the mining camps was very high

An earlier trail followed Harrison and Lillooet (*LIL-ooh-et*) lakes. It fell into disuse once the Cariboo Road was finished. The Cariboo Road was British Columbia's first "highway." It played a key role not just in the gold rush but in the growth of British Columbia generally. Today a paved highway, Highway 97, follows the same route.

Governor James Douglas decided to build a wagon road to the goldfields. Work began at Yale, the southern end of the road, in the spring of 1862. For part of its route the road followed the Fraser River. It had to be carved out of the steep sides of the canyon walls. There was no heavy machinery, so the road was built by hard labour, using explosives to blast a passage through the rock, then pick and shovel to remove the debris.

Wagons hauling supplies on the Cariboo Road high above the Fraser River. This stretch of the road was known as the Great Bluff. After passing over it, one traveller wrote: "no fence whatever and certain death to fall over the precipices into the river." BC Archives A-00350

BC People
THE ROYAL ENGINEERS

Much of the Cariboo Road was planned and built by the Royal Engineers, a troop of soldiers sent out to BC from England in 1858. Besides building roads, the Engineers laid out new townsites, built trails and bridges, and enforced the law. They even had their own brass band, the first one in BC. After four years the Engineers were recalled to England, but many quit the army and stayed in BC to become pioneer settlers.

After three years of construction, the Cariboo Road reached Barkerville. It was 650 kilometres long and had cost well over $1 million (about $20 million in today's money) to build. The road greatly reduced the cost of carrying supplies to the goldfields. Travellers rattled along in stagecoaches pulled by teams of horses. Every few kilometres there was a hotel, called a roadhouse, where travellers could get a meal and a bed to stay overnight.

For fifty years, a familiar sight on the road was the red stage coaches belonging to Frank Barnard's express company, known simply as "the BX." Barnard's stages carried mail, freight, passengers and gold—lots of gold—between Yale and Barkerville. He even had his own ranch, where he raised the finest horses. In winter, sleighs replaced the stagecoaches. The BX was considered to be the longest stage line in North America.

Barkerville: Capital of the Gold Rush

Gold was discovered on the banks of Williams Creek in the heart of the Cariboo Mountains in the summer of 1862. Word got around fast, and a town sprang into being. It was called Barkerville, after Billy Barker, one of the miners who made the big strike.

BC Spotlight
A PROSPECTOR'S TOOLS

A gold pan (A) was like a big soup bowl with sloping sides. A prospector filled the pan with gravel and water, then carefully swirled the contents around. Gold is heavier than rock and gravel, so it sank to the bottom and stayed in the pan when the prospector poured off the water and other material.

A rocker (B) was a wooden box in which the prospector could wash large amounts of sand and gravel. The material was placed on a screen and water was poured over it. When a prospector jiggled the box with a handle, the gold separated from everything else and was caught in riffles, while the water carried away the rest.

A sluice box (C) was a long wooden structure open at both ends. When gravel was shovelled into the sluice and water was passed through it, the gold sank to the bottom and was collected in the riffles.

The prospector used a pickaxe (D) to break up the rock and dig out the pieces of gold.

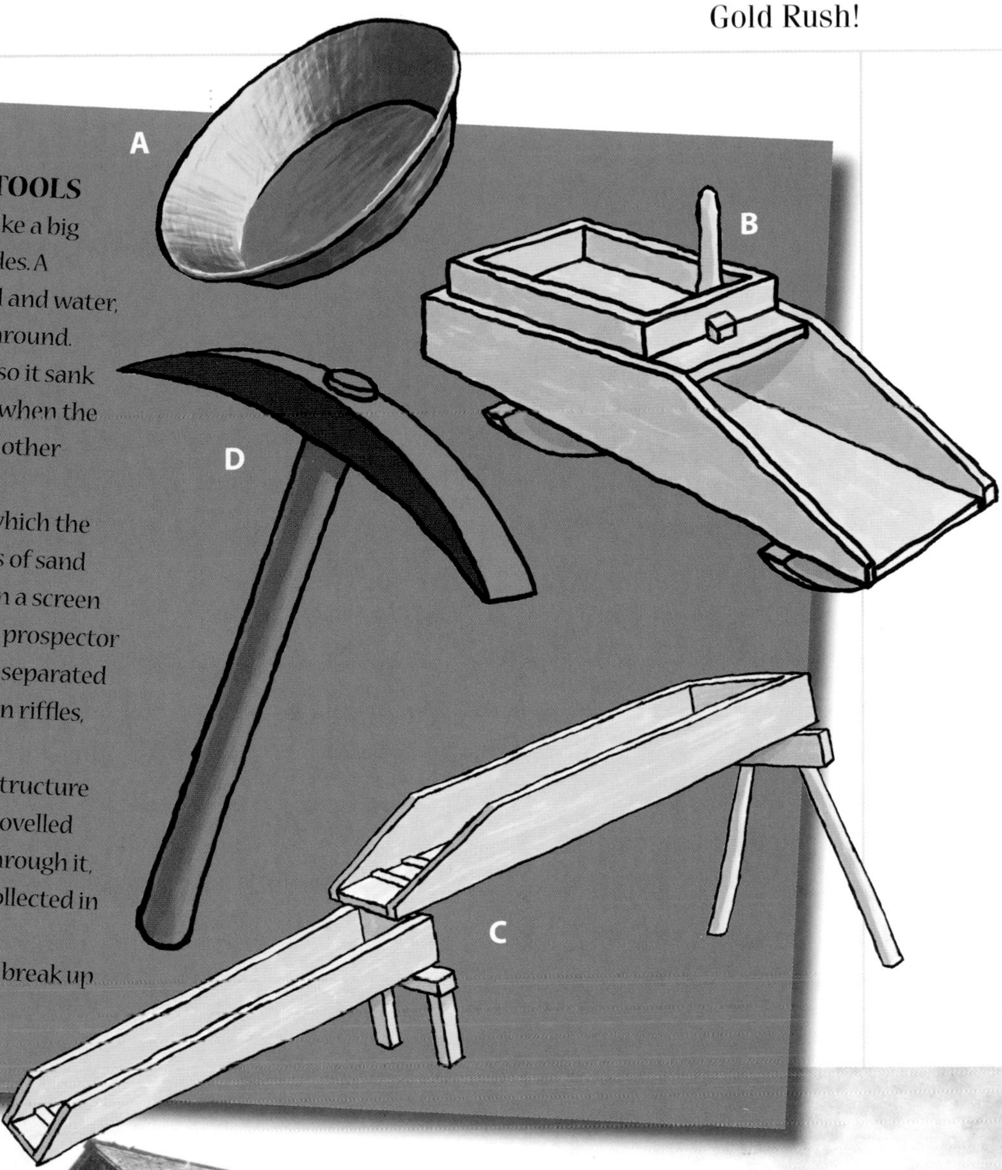

The Clinton Hotel, shown here in 1865, was one of the popular roadhouses on the Cariboo Road, where travellers could stop for a rest. Outside, a pair of freight wagons is waiting to depart. *BC Archives A-03507*

Barkerville was a typical gold rush town. The buildings were thrown together from whatever construction materials were ready at hand. There were general stores, barber shops, laundries, restaurants, blacksmiths, churches, a newspaper and a sawmill. There were also several dance halls and saloons, where the miners came to spend their earnings on liquor and gambling. At one end of town was a Chinatown where the Chinese miners lived. The sidewalks were made of boards and the streets were made of dirt. Animals wandered among the buildings feeding on garbage.

Before long, Barkerville was the largest

Cowboys drive a herd of cattle down the main street of Barkerville in 1868. The animals were imported from the United States to provide meat for hungry miners. But the grasslands of the BC Interior were well suited to grazing cattle, and before long, ranchers were raising animals locally. It was the beginning of the cattle industry in British Columbia. BC Archives A-03787

BC Creatures
CAMELS

Camels? Surely camels live in the desert, not British Columbia. True enough, but during the gold rush, camels made a rare appearance in the Cariboo. The idea came from Frank Laumeister, who made his living packing supplies to the gold camps. He thought that the sure-footed animals would be perfectly suited to BC, so he bought twenty-four of them from the American army. But Laumeister hadn't counted on the camels' smell. The other pack animals—horses and mules—hated it, and ran away whenever a camel came near. Also their feet were too soft for the rocky trails. Laumeister was forced to sell his animals or put them out to pasture, and one by one they died.

BC Archives A-00347

Barkerville as it looks today. Studio Grandell Photography

community north of San Francisco, with a population of ten thousand during the summer mining season. But in September 1868, it was struck by a devastating fire. In less than two hours, most of the town burned to the ground. One eyewitness said that the fire started when a miner tried to kiss one of the girls in a saloon and fell against a stove, and sparks from the chimney set the roof ablaze. The town was rebuilt, but the high point of the gold rush had passed. Prospectors began to drift away to look for gold elsewhere. Barkerville became a ghost town.

In 1958 the government of British Columbia rescued Barkerville. Because it had been such an important place during the gold rush, the government decided to make it a living museum. Workers restored many of the decaying old buildings. Today the entire town looks just as it did during the 1860s. Visitors can chat with actors dressed up as townspeople, stop in at the local saloon, go shopping at the general store and find out how a mine really worked.

The Overlanders

Most prospectors who leapt into the gold rush were Americans, but some came from eastern Canada and made the long trip across the continent to the goldfields. These trekkers, inspired by the hope of striking it rich, were called Overlanders.

In June 1862, a group of 150 Overlanders set off from Fort Garry, Manitoba, to cross the

Catherine Schubert, one of the Overlanders who crossed Canada to seek gold in the 1860s. BC Archives A-03081

Gold Rush!

FAST FACT
In 1862, it took Catherine Schubert and her family 135 days to make the trip from Manitoba to Kamloops.

Plains. Among them was one woman, Catherine Schubert, who was travelling with her husband Augustus and their three children. She was pregnant with a fourth child, but she refused to be left behind.

The Overlanders travelled by cart, horseback and foot. There were no roads, only dusty trails baked by the sun. Every morning they broke camp before dawn and trekked all day. Catherine carried her two babies in baskets slung over the back of a horse. Supplies had to be ferried across the many rivers on makeshift rafts. When rain came, the rivers flooded, turning the prairie into a sea of mud. When they reached the mountains, the travellers struggled up narrow trails and through deep canyons. Their supplies ran out and they had to survive on animals they killed along the way.

At last the Overlanders reached Fort Kamloops. At the First Nations village near the fort, Catherine gave birth to her baby. Then she and Augustus settled at Lillooet, where they cleared land for a farm. While Augustus was

The Mucho Oro ("Lots of Gold") Mine and the men who worked in it. The large wheel is a water wheel, which workers used to empty water that seeped into the mine shafts underground. Note the three Chinese miners on the left. BC Archives A-00613

BC People
PIONEER PHOTOGRAPHERS

Richard Maynard came to BC from Ontario in search of gold. Having no success in the goldfields, he settled in Victoria. In 1862 his wife Hannah joined him there. Richard was a bootmaker by trade and opened a shop in Victoria. Hannah was a photographer, one of the earliest in Canada. She ran her own studio, where people came to have their portraits taken. She taught Richard how to use a camera and in time he, too, became a photographer. Together they ran a successful business for many years.

Left: Hannah and Richard Maynard having their own picture taken. BC Archives A-01507

Below: Hannah and Richard Maynard's "Photographic Gallery and Boot and Shoe Store" in Victoria. BC Archives C-08995

away from home looking for gold, Catherine ran the local school and looked after her children.

Chinese Miners

Among the first boatload of prospectors to arrive in Victoria in 1858 were about thirty Chinese from San Francisco. These pioneers were followed by others, until by the height of the rush almost three thousand Chinese were making a living in British Columbia, a place they called Gold Mountain. Most of them panned for gold in the creeks and riverbeds. They did not have enough money to sink the more permanent underground mines.

Not all of the Chinese newcomers were prospectors. Many were merchants who supplied food and supplies to people in the goldfields. Others ran laundries, restaurants and other businesses. Still others worked as labourers on the Cariboo Road and other construction projects. In Victoria, Yale, Quesnel and Barkerville, they settled in their own neighbourhoods, called Chinatowns.

The Chinese suffered prejudice at the hands of white pioneers. They received lower pay for their work, and sometimes the other miners tried to keep them away from the diggings by force. But the Chinese miners were hardworking. They often found gold where other miners had already given up. In time, many earned enough to bring their families to live in British Columbia. These early pioneers

FAST FACT
None of the Overlanders ever struck it rich in the goldfields, but many remained in British Columbia, where they built successful careers.

formed the beginning of what is today the province's large Chinese community.

Creation of a Colony

When the American miners first arrived, Governor Douglas worried that the goldfields might become part of the United States. To stop this from happening, the British government declared the mainland to be a British colony in 1858. Douglas was now governor of two colonies: Vancouver Island and British Columbia.

Governor Douglas took steps to create a stable society in British Columbia. He appointed officials to enforce the laws. He built roads to the Interior and established towns. He was assisted by Judge Matthew Baillie Begbie, a stern, bearded man who travelled from mining camp to mining camp making sure that laws were being obeyed and peace was maintained. They called him "the "Hanging Judge" because he did not hesitate to punish lawbreakers, but he was respected for being honest and fair.

The colony attracted mainly men to its mining camps and fur-trade posts. There was very little family life because there were so few women. Some of the newcomers took First Nations wives. But church and government leaders wanted to establish a European society in the colony. One answer was to import women from Britain. In 1862, several dozen young women arrived from London aboard two ships, called "bride ships." The plan was that they would work as servants and schoolteachers and eventually marry. Some of these women were widows whose husbands had died and left

In Their Own Words
JUDGE BEGBIE
Judge Matthew Begbie once told a group of miners:
Boys, I'm here to keep order and administer the law. Those who don't want law and order can git. For boys, if there is shooting, there will be hanging.

them in need. Others were working women who sought adventure or opportunity in the new colony. Still others were orphans, or young girls whose parents were too poor to look after them. In the end, most of them did marry and raise families.

The gold rush reached its peak in 1863, when about 10 tonnes of gold came out of the Cariboo creeks. After that the excitement began to cool down. Prospectors slowly began to drift away to search for other strikes, or to take up other professions.

But the gold rush changed British Columbia forever. It brought the first settlers to the mainland and led to the development of many communities. It provided customers for merchants, ranchers and farmers. A transportation network was built to connect the Interior to the coast. A legal system, a mail service and a police force were all put in place. British Columbia was ready for the next stage in its development.

The Canadian Pacific Railway, completed in 1885, connected British Columbia to the rest of Canada beyond the mountains. *City of Vancouver Archives. LGN 638*

JOINING CANADA

4

Faced with a decision, people in British Columbia debated their future. Should they join the United States, or remain a colony of Great Britain? In the end they decided to join the new country of Canada that was taking shape on the other side of the mountains.

Union of the Colonies

Mainland British Columbia was created as a colony separate from Vancouver Island in 1858. The experiment soon turned out to be a financial failure. The construction of the Cariboo Wagon Road and all the other public works that followed the gold rush cost a lot of money. Both colonies were deeply in debt, and they were not attracting enough settlers to raise money from taxes or the sale of land. It seemed a waste to spend money running two separate governments. In 1866, the colony of Vancouver Island merged with the mainland, forming a single colony called British Columbia.

As a colony, British Columbia was expected to send valuable goods and services to Great Britain, the "mother country." This was the way the great European powers all over the world ran their colonies. Trade goods from overseas brought much wealth to the countries of Europe. British Columbia, for example, produced gold and furs, and thanks to its location on the Pacific Ocean, it was a handy base for Great Britain's naval fleet. The lush forests provided tall, straight timber to build ships and masts. When coal was discovered on Vancouver Island, mines were developed to provide fuel for the new coal-fired steam engines that were being installed on British ships. Then, in 1862, the British navy decided to move its headquarters in the Pacific from Chile to Esquimalt (*Es-KWY-malt*), a protected harbour next door to Victoria. Ever since, Esquimalt has been an important naval base.

In return for these benefits, Great Britain paid for the battleships and soldiers to defend

Joining Canada

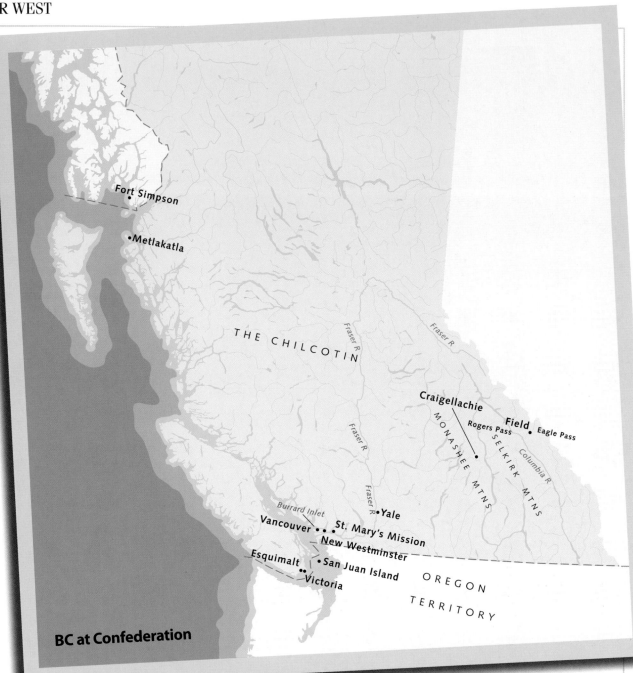

Fort Simpson

•Metlakatla

THE CHILCOTIN

Fraser R

Fraser R

Craigellachie

Field •Eagle Pass

Rogers Pass

MONASHEE MTNS

SELKIRK MTNS

Columbia R

Fraser R

Fraser R •Yale

Burrard Inlet

Vancouver • •

St. Mary's Mission

New Westminster

Esquimalt

• San Juan Island

Victoria

OREGON

TERRITORY

BC at Confederation

its colony and paid the cost of running the government. But increasingly, colonists in British Columbia grew unhappy with this arrangement. The world was changing around them. The gold was running out. The colony was deep in debt. Jobs were scarce, and businesses were going broke.

British Columbians had to make a decision about their future. They felt that they had three options:

1. To become Americans. The colony was squeezed between two American territories:

Oregon to the south and Alaska, purchased by the United States in 1867, to the north. Many residents were Americans by birth who had come to BC for the gold rush. The United States had a large, prosperous economy and, by 1862, a railway running right across the continent.

2. To become Canadians. Across the Rocky Mountains the new Dominion of Canada, created in 1867 by joining four eastern provinces, was spreading across the Interior of the country. There was talk of a new railway running all the way to the Pacific, which could be a good deal for British Columbia.

The waterfront at New Westminster in 1860. The ship is the Vickeray from San Francisco, the first vessel to load cargo at the little port. BC Archives B-06377

BC Places

THE FIRST CAPITAL

When the new mainland colony was created, a new city was founded on the banks of the Fraser River, on the site of a former Aboriginal village, and designated as the capital. At first it was named Queensborough, but Queen Victoria chose to call it New Westminster instead. When the two colonies joined in 1866, New Westminster remained the capital of British Columbia for two years until the seat of government moved to Victoria. At this time someone remarked that New Westminster was "nothing more than a small village built among the stumps of the forest."

Joining Canada

Amor de Cosmos, a feisty, dedicated politician, 1865.
BC Archives A-01224

3. To leave things the way they were. A small number of people were deeply attached to Great Britain. Many of them were officials in the old government who feared they would lose their positions under a new regime.

Confederation

The faction of British Columbians in favour of joining Canada was led by Amor de Cosmos, a fiery newspaper editor and politician. In 1868, he and some allies formed the Confederation League to build support for union with Canada. Their movement got a boost when Great Britain sent a new governor to coax BC residents into Confederation.

It soon became clear that most settlers favoured union with Canada, but not union

BC People
LOVER OF THE UNIVERSE

One of the most unusual politicians British Columbia, or any other place, has ever seen was Bill Smith—or, as he was more commonly known, Amor de Cosmos.

Smith was born in Nova Scotia, and like many others he was attracted west by the gold rush. When he moved to California in search of gold, he decided he needed a new name for a new country. He chose Amor de Cosmos, which means "Lover of the Universe."

After he moved north to BC, de Cosmos started a newspaper in Victoria and got involved in politics. He was a passionate speaker who often got so carried away that he began whacking opponents on the head with his walking stick. He thought the voting public should have more power, instead of appointed officials. He also supported union with Canada and worked tirelessly for the cause.

Following Confederation, he was elected to parliament in Ottawa, then served a term as premier of British Columbia. When he tried to change the terms under which BC entered the union, an angry mob burst into the legislature threatening to lynch him. De Cosmos was forced to flee through a side door. Four days later he resigned as premier.

In his later years he lived a lonely life as a recluse. He became quite eccentric and people shied away from him in the street. Still, de Cosmos is remembered as a fierce defender of democracy. As much as anyone, he was responsible for British Columbia joining Canada.

at any price. In 1870, three delegates travelled to Ottawa to negotiate the terms under which British Columbia would become a province of Canada. They asked that Canada take over BC's bulging debt and pay the new province a sum of money each year. They wanted a wagon road built across the Prairies to the west coast. And they asked for a more democratic form of government. Much to the surprise of the delegates, the Canadians not only agreed to these terms, they promised to build a railway instead of a wagon road.

Back home in BC, the delegation was applauded for its work. Elections were held to find out how residents felt. The result was a complete victory for the supporters of Confederation, and British Columbians accepted the Canadians' offer quickly. On July 20, 1871, British Columbia became Canada's sixth province.

At the time of Confederation in 1871, British Columbia was a rough frontier outpost. Many of the residents had come from Britain and tried to create a small model of the mother country far from home. This fashionable group in Victoria has just enjoyed a game of lawn tennis. To this day, Victoria keeps some of its British flavour. BC Archives C-03924

WHEN CANADA'S PROVINCES JOINED CONFEDERATION

Ontario	1867
Quebec	1867
Nova Scotia	1867
New Brunswick	1867
Manitoba	1870
British Columbia	1871
Prince Edward Island	1873
Alberta	1905
Saskatchewan	1905
Newfoundland/Labrador	1949

The government of the new province was elected, but not by all British Columbians, because not everyone was permitted to vote. For one thing, politics was considered men's

business. No women were allowed to take part in elections, not for many years. Neither were all men. In order to qualify, a man had to be twenty-one years of age or older; he had to have lived in BC for at least six months; and he had to be able to read and write. Furthermore, people of different ethnic backgrounds were excluded. In 1874, Aboriginal and Chinese people lost the vote; so did Japanese-born people in 1895 and South Asians in 1907. These people were not allowed to take part in elections for many years.

WHEN THEY WERE ALLOWED TO VOTE IN PROVINCIAL ELECTIONS

Women	1917
Chinese Canadians	1947
South Asian Canadians	1947
Japanese Canadians	1949
Aboriginals	1949

Disease and Defiance

At the time of Confederation, about 25,000 Aboriginal people were living in the new province. That was many more than the non-Aboriginal population, but far fewer than the number of Aboriginals who had lived there only a few years earlier. Most of them had been killed by disease. Native people in North America had no resistance to the common illnesses brought to their land by Europeans. Epidemics of measles and smallpox, such as the devastating smallpox epidemic of 1862, swept away whole villages.

The survivors tried to adjust to the arrival of settlers in their lands, but it was difficult. The newcomers had little respect for Aboriginal ways of life. They did not understand how people could make their living from hunting and fishing, and they did not understand the deep attachment that Native people had to the land. Between 1850 and 1854, James Douglas,

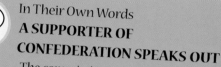

In Their Own Words

A SUPPORTER OF CONFEDERATION SPEAKS OUT

The commissioner of lands and works, Joseph Trutch, explained why he supported Confederation with Canada:

I advocate Confederation because it will secure the continuance of this Colony under the British Flag, and strengthen British interests on this Continent; and because it will benefit this community, by lessening taxation and giving increased revenue for local expenditure; by advancing the political status of the Colony; by securing the aid of the Dominion Government, who are, I believe, able to carry into effect measures tending to develop the natural resources, and to promote the prosperity of this Colony; and by affording, through a railway, the only means of acquiring a permanent population, which must come from east of the Rocky Mountains.

the governor of British Columbia, made agreements with several Aboriginal tribes on Vancouver Island. In return for blankets, small reserves (land set aside for them) and the promise that they could go on hunting and fishing, the tribes gave up their land to the newcomers. But these were the only agreements made in British Columbia for many years. For the most part, settlers did not ask permission before taking possession of Aboriginal territory and imposing new forms of law and government.

From time to time, Aboriginal people fought back. In 1864, a group of Tsilhqot'in (Chilcotin) attacked a road crew as it tried to build a road across the Chilcotin plateau in the central Interior. It is not known for sure what caused the local people to take up arms. Apparently, members of the building crew were mistreating them. The Tsilhqot'in may also have been fighting to protect their land from the intruders. Whatever the cause, a group of soldiers marched to the area, arrested the murderers and, after a trial, hanged them.

Similar acts of rebellion against the newcomers took place on the coast. And similarly the authorities responded with cannons and gunboats, forcing the tribes to give up their resistance.

The ways of the Aboriginal people were not the ways of the settlers, and so the settlers mistrusted them and shut them out of the new society they were creating. For the time being at least, Aboriginal people were treated as outsiders in their own land.

At War Over a Pig

Lyman Cutler was an American farmer who lived on San Juan Island, one of the islands lying between the mainland and the south end of Vancouver Island. One day in June 1859, a pig wandered onto his land from a neighbouring farm. Cutler shot the pig—and almost started a war.

The dead pig belonged to the Hudson's Bay Company, which owned the farm next door. The Company wanted to be paid for its loss and a judge was sent from Victoria to settle the matter. In response, American soldiers arrived to protect the rights of American citizens. Soon

A group of Aboriginal leaders at St. Mary's Mission on the Fraser River, 1867. BC Archives O-09263

In Their Own Words
KING-GEORGE-MEN

One Aboriginal elder spoke for all his people when he said:

We see your ships and hear things that make our hearts grow faint. They say that more King-George-men [whites] will soon be here, and will take our land, our firewood, our fishing grounds; that we shall be placed on a little spot, and shall do everything according to the fancies of the King-George-men.

William Duncan with Tsimshian children of Metlakatla. BC Archives A-01067

BC People
WILLIAM DUNCAN OF METLAKATLA

To the outside world, there was no place in British Columbia more famous than a small village far away on the north coast. Every visitor wanted to take the steamboat to Metlakatla (*Met-lah-KAT-lah*). What they saw astounded them. There were paved sidewalks lit by street lamps, a bustling sawmill, a firehall, a jail, a salmon cannery and the largest church north of San Francisco. It was, in the words of one tourist, "just like an English village."

What astonished the visitors was that the residents of Metlakatla were all local Tsimshian (*SIM-shan*) people. They had been led to Metlakatla by an English missionary, William Duncan. He came to the Tsimshian in 1857 to teach them about Christianity. Like other missionaries who came to BC, he did not think that Aboriginal religious beliefs had any value. He felt that Christianity was the only true religion, and that it was his duty to spread it to all the Aboriginal people.

Duncan set to work at Fort Simpson. But he grew discouraged. The Tsimshian kept to their old ways and did not accept the new religion. Duncan decided the answer was to move to an isolated location, away from the trading fort. It was at this time that the terrible smallpox epidemic swept up the coast toward Fort Simpson. Duncan, who had medicine that would fight the smallpox, told the people that if they came with him, they would be safe. Several hundred Tsimshian followed him, and together they built the village of Metlakatla.

Residents of Metlakatla had to obey strict rules. They had to give up their old religious beliefs and ceremonies. They had to stop drinking alcohol, gambling and painting their faces. All children had to attend school, and everyone had to rest on Sundays and attend church faithfully. The people even had to pay taxes: $2.50 a year, or a blanket.

Duncan ran Metlakatla as if it were his own private country. He took orders from no one, which made him unpopular with officials in his church. After twenty-five years he decided it was time to move. Along with about 800 people from the village, he moved north into Alaska and established a new community. The old Metlakatla disappeared back into the forest.

British warships were cruising offshore, and Britain and the United States stood at the brink of war.

Obviously, the issue was much bigger than just a pig. The dispute was really over who owned San Juan Island. Was it part of British Columbia, or part of the United States? No one knew for sure. The border between the two follows the 49th parallel of latitude between the Rocky Mountains and the Pacific. When it reaches the ocean, the border dips south through Georgia Strait and around the bottom of Vancouver Island. But a maze of islands lies in the strait, San Juan Island being one of them. No one had ever decided for certain on which side of the border the islands lay.

In the end, war was averted. The island was shared until the true border could be decided. Many years after Lyman Cutler shot his neighbour's pig, the United States took official possession of San Juan Island.

Finding a Route

British Columbia had entered Confederation on the promise that a railway would be built linking the province to central and eastern Canada. But the railway was slow in coming. Politicians in Ottawa complained about the cost and tried to delay it. They called British Columbia "the spoiled child of Confederation"

An argument over a pig nearly touched off a battle with the US.

for demanding such an expensive project. This angered people west of the mountains, who began to wonder why they had bothered to join Confederation.

While the politicians argued, work on the railway did go ahead. The first step was to decide what route the track would follow. British Columbia was a sea of mountains from

Sandford Fleming (second from left) was the engineer in charge of the new railway. Here he is in 1872, just before setting off with some companions to cross the country in search of possible routes. National Archives of Canada C-002787

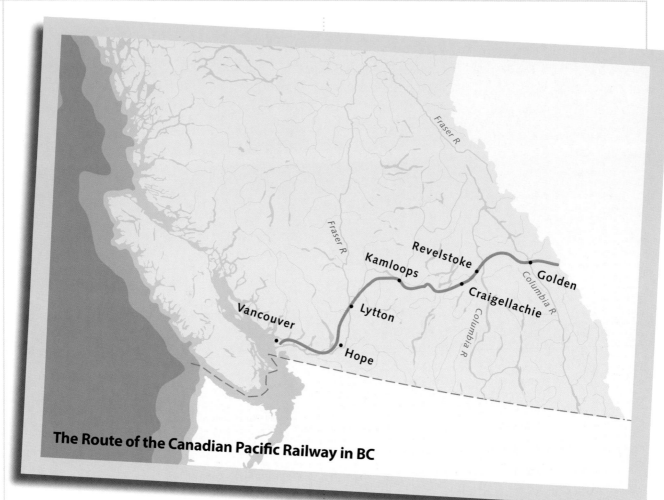

The Route of the Canadian Pacific Railway in BC

the Rockies to the coast. The only way through was the footpaths used by the Aboriginal people and a few rough wagon roads made by the gold miners. "It is going to cost you money to get through those canyons," one surveyor said. He was right.

Finding a route through the mountains was a job for the surveyors. They were trained engineers, but they were also adventurers. They trekked through parts of the country that no white person had ever seen before, climbing tall mountains and wading across raging streams. One of these surveyors, Walter Moberly, found a pass through the Monashee Mountains. He called it Eagle Pass because he was drawn to it by following the flight of some of these majestic birds. Another surveyor was Major A.B. Rogers. His discovery of a route through the Selkirk Mountains is now called Rogers Pass.

Building the Railway

Finally, after a decade of dickering, British Columbia got its railway. A new company was formed to build it—the Canadian Pacific Railway Company, the CPR. In BC, construction began on May 15, 1880, at the town of Yale in the canyon of the Fraser River. Yale was as far up the river as steamboats could carry supplies from the coast before the rapids stopped them. From there, the old Cariboo Road was used to haul building materials to the construction site.

The person in charge of building the western section of the line was Andrew Onderdonk, an engineer from New York. The challenge he had accepted was immense. He had to push a rail line along the steep walls of the Fraser River and through the mountains of the Interior. On the flat prairies, rail builders were laying track at a rate of 10 kilometres every day. In the Fraser Canyon, it took eighteen months just to blast four tunnels along a 2.5-kilometre stretch.

A century ago there were no machines to build the line—no bulldozers, cranes or trucks. Everything had to be done by workers using picks and shovels and horse-drawn wagons. The route followed the banks of the major rivers, but these banks were steep and rocky. At some places workers were lowered on ropes over the side of the canyon to place dynamite charges for blasting. They worked in bare feet to get the best footing. Hundreds of wooden bridges carried the track across the deep gorges. Workers got so fast at building these bridges it was said that trains would run across a bridge in the evening that was made of timbers that had been trees just that morning.

One of the greatest challenges was the Big Hill. This was a very steep incline in the Rocky Mountains near the town of Field. It was almost 13 kilometres long, and steeper than any other section of railway track in the world. Four powerful engines were needed to pull a train to the summit. The first train to travel down the

In Their Own Words
HUSTLE AND BUSTLE

A visitor described Yale, BC, in the 1880s during railway construction:

People don't walk in Yale, they rush. From peep o'day 'til long into the night the movement of men, horses, and wagons along the street goes on.

A dance out here means business. The last one commenced at 12 o'clock on Monday morning and lasted continuously day and night until 12 o'clock the next Saturday.

Building a cantilever bridge going west. Canadian Pacific Railway, near Cisco Flat south of Lytton, Fraser River, 1884. BC Archives D-08738

FAST FACT
Some railway workers suffered from scurvy, a disease that causes bleeding gums and bruises that don't heal. Scurvy is caused by a lack of Vitamin C, which is found in fresh fruit and vegetables.

other side went out of control and plunged into the river at the bottom, killing three people. Special brakes were used on the downward run, and the trains crept along at slow speed. It was twenty years before the railway reduced the danger by replacing the Big Hill with a series of tunnels through the mountains.

Chinese Workers

Faced with a shortage of workers, Onderdonk imported about seventeen thousand Chinese labourers to work on the railway. They were paid $1 a day, less than half what the other workers received. The foremen gave the Chinese the most dangerous job of laying dynamite to blast a path through the rock. About 600 Chinese workers died, crushed in landslides, blown up in explosions or sick with scurvy in the camps.

Without the Chinese, the railway might not

A Chinese work gang takes a rest from the backbreaking labour of building the railway, 1880s. Glenbow Archives NA3740-29

have been built at all—it would have been too expensive. Yet they were considered transients, allowed in to the country only to build the line. When they were no longer needed, they were simply laid off. Once the railway was finished, the government introduced laws making it very difficult for Chinese to enter Canada.

The Creation of Vancouver

Vancouver began as a port—a small group of shacks huddled around a sawmill on the shores of Burrard Inlet. Ships from around the world came to the mill to load lumber. The tiny logging village was called Granville. It was also known as Gastown after its most famous resident, the gossipy tavern keeper "Gassy Jack" Deighton.

Then, in 1884, the CPR decided to build the railway to the shores of Burrard Inlet at Granville. This would make it easier to exchange cargo between the trains and sea-going vessels from Asia and Australia. Two years later the city was established as Vancouver, named for the British explorer Captain George Vancouver.

Less than three months after it was born, Vancouver was almost destroyed. On June 13,

Gastown in 1885. In a year's time the sleepy sawmill village would become the City of Vancouver and be transformed by the arrival of the Canadian Pacific Railway. Gordon Miller painting

1886, a great fire swept through the settlement. At least eleven people died, and most of the wooden buildings were reduced to ashes.

But there was no destroying Vancouver. The fire took place on Sunday. By Wednesday, a brand new three-storey hotel was open for business and many other buildings were under construction. On May 23, 1887, the first passenger train arrived from Montreal and Canada's port on the Pacific was bursting with activity.

The Last Spike

While Onderdonk and his workers were building the railway from the coast toward the Interior, other crews were building west across the mountains from the plains. The two ends met in the middle of the province at a place called Craigellachie (*Kraig-a-LATCH-ee*) on November 7, 1885. The president of the railway, Donald Smith, came out from Montreal. In front of a small group of dignitaries, he hammered the last spike into the track to complete the job. The dream of a railway running right across the continent from Montreal to Vancouver was now a reality.

The railway had a profound impact on British Columbia. It was an iron thread attaching the Pacific province to the rest of Canada. All along the route, towns sprang into life. Vancouver, the western terminus of the line, grew into a

This is what Gastown looked like before the great fire of 1886 burned almost all of it to the ground. In the distance, ships come and go at the Hastings sawmill, the little town's main employer. The mill was one of the few buildings to survive the fire. The morning after the blaze supplies began arriving to begin the rebuilding job, and a new city quickly rose from the ashes. Today this area is the historic downtown Gastown neighbourhood. Gordon Miller painting

The railway connected British Columbia to the rest of Canada. Here is the first train between Montreal and the BC coast, 1886. Denley, Norman, Library and Archives Canada PA-066579

bustling port city. Wheat from the Prairies was carried out to the coast to be exported by ship around the world. In the other direction, timber from coastal forests was carried to the Prairies to build homes for the new settlers arriving there. The money BC had received from Canada to build the railway gave a boost to the local economy. It seemed to British Columbians that they had chosen wisely by deciding to make their future as Canadians.

These photographs show two versions of the last spike ceremony at Craigellachie. The official ceremony is pictured on the top opposite. It shows Donald Smith, president of the railway, getting ready to hammer in the spike. The photograph on the bottom left shows a group of workers gathered together to have their own ceremony after the bigwigs had left. BC Archives A-01744 and Canadian Pacific Railway Archives A.1340

This painting shows the Canadian Pacific wharf on the Vancouver waterfront on a busy day in 1887. A freight train is arriving from Eastern Canada. So is a coastal steamboat, bringing mail and passengers from Victoria. *Gordon Miller painting*

RESOURCES AND THE ECONOMY

5

From the earliest days, British Columbians have relied for their livelihood on the resources of the land and sea. This was true of the Aboriginal people, just as it was true of later settlers. Fish, timber and minerals were three of the province's richest resources. They became the foundation of British Columbia's wealth.

Harvest from the Sea

For thousands of years, the First People of British Columbia relied on fish for food and trade. When the new settlers moved into the province, they immediately recognized the value of the fishery, not only for their own use but also as a source of products that could be sold to customers around the world.

Before salmon could be shipped to other countries for sale, a way had to be found to keep it fresh so that it wouldn't spoil before it reached the market. The Hudson's Bay Company made the first attempt to export fish. The company bought salmon from Aboriginal fishers, then salted it in barrels for shipment to Hawaii.

Canning was introduced in the 1870s. Fish packed in cans could be cooked to last a long time and was easy to handle for export. Many

Men working with dried salmon on the Steveston Wharf, 1908. Vancouver Public Library Special Collections 2142

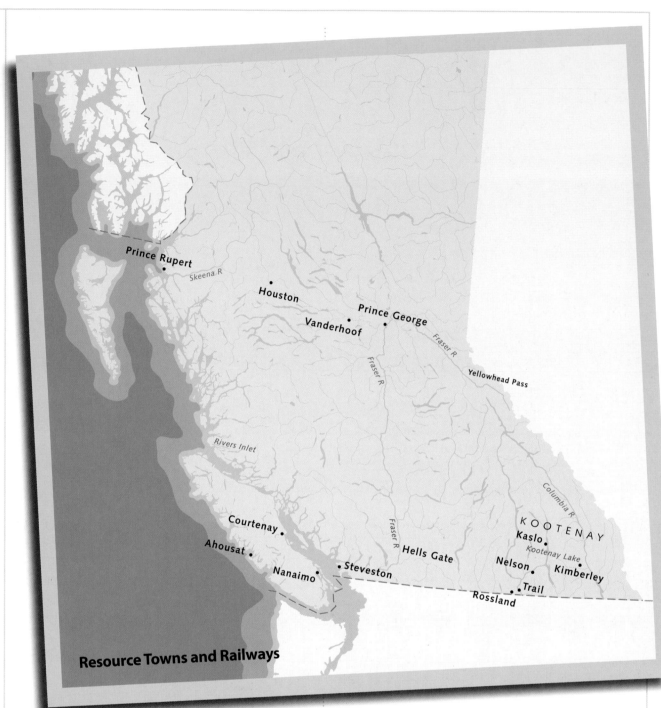

Resource Towns and Railways

canneries went into operation at the mouth of the Fraser River, then all along the coast to the north. By the 1920s, more than fifty canneries were operating along the coast of British Columbia.

Inside the Cannery

Canneries were huge factories where hundreds of people worked. The fish were gutted, cleaned and chopped up at long tables.

Meanwhile, other crews made the cans from sheets of tin. The cans were filled with pieces of fish, soldered shut, then heated in huge pressure cookers to cook the contents. Afterwards, labels were pasted on the cans and they were packed in cases ready for shipping.

FAST FACT
Using a razor-sharp knife, a skilled butcher could process 2,000 salmon during a 10-hour workday.

Salmon from British Columbia ended up in kitchens around the world as far away as Great Britain and Australia. Sockeye in particular was popular with consumers, who loved its rich, red colour and delicious taste.

The fishery was a vast United Nations of people from different backgrounds. Many Japanese and Aboriginal people were fishers. Inside the cannery, the workers were mainly Chinese and Aboriginal women. Children also worked in the canneries doing menial jobs.

Canneries were only open during the summer season, from about May to October, when the salmon returned to the rivers. At this time Aboriginal people came from all over the coast to live at the canneries. Families occupied separate cabins or camps, called rancheries.

These First Nations women worked in the cannery at Alert Bay in the early 1900s. Many of the workers were Chinese and Aboriginal women. There were no daycare centres or kindergartens. Women with small babies brought them right into the cannery. BC Archives F-07419

BC People
WEST COAST BOYHOOD

Earl Maquinna George grew up in the village of Ahousat (*ah-HOW-sat*) on the west coast of Vancouver Island, a member of the Nuu-chah-nulth people. When he was a young boy, his parents travelled in the summer up the coast to Rivers Inlet to work in the salmon canneries. They took young Earl along with them. "We reached Rivers Inlet with 300 or 400 other boats that were going fishing like we were," he recalled. "A lot of them had men and women and children who were going to work in the cannery."

Just twelve years old, Earl was hired to work in the cannery. It was his first experience on the job. He carried baskets of empty cans to the women who filled them with salmon. He was paid 13 cents an hour, and sometimes had to work seventeen hours a day. Meanwhile, his father and his younger brother went fishing. The family stayed in Rivers Inlet for the fishing season, then returned home with their earnings. This is how many First Nations families made a living on the coast.

Gillnetters at work near the mouth of the Fraser River around 1910. Sometimes fishers stayed out in these small boats for several days. BC Archives B-08416

The Chinese lived in their own bunkhouses, known as Chinahouses, where each worker had a small cubicle with a bed and a table. When the canning season ended, Aboriginal workers returned to their villages, while the Chinese found other kinds of work as farm labourers, mill hands, miners or storekeepers. Only caretakers remained at the silent canneries.

Fishing for a Living

Each cannery was supplied with fish by its own fleet of fish boats. These boats dropped their nets or set their fishing lines at the mouths of the rivers to catch the salmon as they passed—millions of them—on their way upriver to spawn. During the day, scows came from the canneries to collect the fish that had

---

In Their Own Words
CANOES ARRIVING

As a teenage boy, Edwin DeBeck would watch the Aboriginal workers arrive at the canneries at Steveston, south of Vancouver.

Well here they come on a flood tide in the late afternoon bowling along ahead of a westerly wind. Great canoes 50 feet [15 m] and over, each with 4 sails. Some came all the way from the Skeena and the Queen Charlottes. They came in a flotilla, about 12 of the big ones and an equal number of lesser ones about 40 feet [12 m] or a little less. I'm sure one of the big canoes could hold up to 100 if you counted children but did not count dogs…

There was considerable ceremony to the landing. A few hundred yards out sails were lowered and they started singing Indian songs until they got close to the wharf. With a final shout a sudden silence. Dead silence for about a minute. Then the biggest chief stood and with a speaking staff in his hand made a short speech. A sudden stop. A barked order. And then all hell broke loose. Everyone seemed to be rushing here and there.

been caught. The earliest fishers powered their boats with sails and oars, so they could not venture far from the cannery. When gasoline motors became available in about 1910, boats were able to go farther offshore.

Fishers used three different techniques for catching fish. Some boats used gillnets, mesh nets with weights at the bottom and cork floats along the top so that they hang in the water like a wall. Fish swim into the net, get their gills entangled in the mesh and cannot escape. In the early days, nets were hauled back into the boat by hand, a backbreaking job.

Other boats were seiners (*SAYN-ers*). They used larger nets that were played out behind the boat in a circle. When the circle was closed, the bottom of the net was tightened to form a bag, or purse. Fish caught within the circle could not escape.

The third method was trolling (*TROE-ling*). Instead of nets, trollers used a series of lines, each set with several baited hooks. Boats dragged several lines at once slowly through the water, waiting for the fish to strike.

Today, gillnetting, seining and trolling are still the three main techniques used by fishers on the Pacific coast.

Another Railway to the Sea

Charles Hays was a railway executive in Canada, the president of the Grand Trunk Pacific Railway (GTPR), a company that was building a second rail line across the country to the Pacific. The GTPR crossed the Great Plains in the north and took the Yellowhead Pass through the Rocky Mountains into BC. Then

BC Places
STEVESTON
The centre of the canning industry was Steveston, a community at the mouth of the Fraser River. It was known as the Sockeye Capital of the World. A visitor in 1901 described the town: "There are twenty-nine canneries at this queer town of plank streets, wooden houses and big canneries that straggle all along the river front. It is alive and kicking for two or three months in the year—the rest of the time it sleeps, and the visitor wanders through deserted thoroughfares and shut up canneries."

This photograph shows the canneries lining the waterfront at Steveston in about 1913. BC Archives E-00091

The Route of the Grand Trunk Pacific Railway

Arrival of the first train from Winnipeg to Prince Rupert, 1914. BC Archives A-00489

Railway construction at Prince George, 1914.
BC Archives B-00312

it wound across the centre of the province and down the valley of the Skeena River until it arrived at the brand new city of Prince Rupert on the coast.

Hays had great plans for Prince Rupert. He foresaw the day when it would become a major seaport with ships arriving from around the world. But then, in April 1912, disaster struck in the Atlantic Ocean. The giant liner *Titanic*, on its first voyage out of England on the way to New York, steamed into an iceberg. The *Titanic* was supposed to be unsinkable, but the berg smashed a hole in its steel hull and the vessel sank. More than 1,500 passengers drowned, and Charles Hays was one of them.

Some say Hays's dreams went down with him on the *Titanic*. Prince Rupert did not develop the way he had hoped. The GTPR, completed in 1914, soon went bankrupt and had to be rescued by the government. However,

the rail line did provide access to and from the north-central part of the province. And many Interior communities, including Prince George, Vanderhoof, Houston and others, owe their origins to the coming of the Grand Trunk Pacific.

Disappearing Fish

In the early years of the colony of British Columbia, there were so many salmon that it seemed as if they would last forever. Nobody gave any thought to preserving their numbers. Vast quantities were wasted every year—simply thrown away at the canneries because they could not be used—but millions of fish returned to the rivers.

Then disaster struck. At the narrow gorge along the Fraser River known as Hells Gate, the fish fought their way up powerful rapids on their way to spawning grounds in the Interior. In 1913, railway builders were laying track beside the river through Hells Gate and their blasting caused rock slides into the river, making it

Resources and the Economy

BC Creatures
THE STORY OF SALMON

The early fishing industry in British Columbia depended on the salmon. This was the most popular fish with consumers in eastern Canada and Europe.

Salmon are born, or spawned, in the rivers and lakes of the Interior of British Columbia. As the young fish grow in size, they migrate down the waterways to the Pacific Ocean, where they adapt to life in salt water. For several years they wander far and wide across the Pacific. When it is time for them to give birth, they return to the freshwater places where they began. By a miracle of nature, each fish finds its way back to the exact same stream where it was born. There it completes the cycle by producing its own young, then dying.

impossible for the fish to pass. Millions of fish died, unable to spawn. It was thirty years before the damage was repaired. Even then the Fraser never again produced as many salmon as it did before the slides.

The fishers and the cannery owners soon realized that steps had to be taken to slow down the slaughter. They wanted to keep on profiting from the fishery and the cannery supplied many jobs. However, they also realized that if the salmon disappeared, there would be no industry at all. The history of the salmon fishery ever since has been an attempt to balance people's need for food with the long-term survival of the fish.

Tall Timber

Another important resource from British Columbia was wood. Most of the province was cloaked in thick forests of tall timber. Visitors were awed by the size of the trees.

Aboriginal people made the tall cedar trees into totem poles, canoes and planks for their houses. Later, the British navy used the trees for masts for their sailing vessels. Then, as settlers moved into the province in greater numbers, the demand for lumber grew even more. Everything was made of wood in those days: houses, ships, buildings of all types, even sidewalks.

Working in the Woods

Logging began first along the coast, where timber grew especially tall and was easy to reach and transport. Loggers felled the trees on the steep slopes, then rolled them down into the water. These men were called handloggers because they had no machinery; everything was done by muscle power. Where land was flat, logs were hauled to the water by teams of horses or oxen. Floating logs were joined together in large rafts, called booms, and towed down the coast to the nearest sawmill for cutting into lumber.

The arrival of the railway made a big difference to the loggers. Track was laid into the woods and special logging railways carried logs to the water, or directly to sawmills. Railways also made it possible to bring logs out of the Interior, and logging spread throughout the province.

In Their Own Words
DAVID THOMPSON

The explorer David Thompson wrote: "We are pygmies among the giant pines and cedars of this country."

In the forests of British Columbia, trees grow as tall as 30-storey buildings. It took the early loggers many hours of hard work with axes and hand saws to chop one down, as in this photograph taken by Mattie Gunterman in the 1890s. *Vancouver Public Library Special collections 1803*

A LOGGER'S DAY

An early handlogger described the daily routine in one of the coastal camps about 1900:

The first morning light would see them already at their place of work, perhaps a mile's rowboat journey from their home. There they would slave all day; carrying their sharp, awkward tools up through the hillside underbrush; chopping and sawing, felling big timber; cutting up logs, barking them; using their heavy jackscrews to coax logs downhill to the sea. At evening, they would tow such logs as they had floated round to their boom, and put the logs inside, in safety. Then they could go home and dry their clothes, and cook supper, and sleep like dead men.

From *Woodsmen of the West*, M.A. Grainger (Arnold, 1908), p. 53.

BC People

FRENCH IN THE WEST

French-speaking people from Quebec have lived in British Columbia ever since the days of the fur trade. Most of the voyageurs returned to Quebec when their tour of duty in the West ended, but a few remained and became British Columbia's first French residents.

The logging industry brought another influx of French speakers. In 1909, a sawmill owner in New Westminster imported 150 workers from Quebec to operate his mill. Logging was an important activity in Quebec as well, and the owner knew that he would be getting experienced workers.

The Quebec workers settled together in houses north of the mill. Others followed, and pretty soon there was a French-speaking community of families centred around a Catholic church. It took its name from the priest, Edmond Maillard.

Today many more French-speaking people live all over British Columbia, but the pioneering community of Maillardville (*ma-LARD-vill*) still keeps its French character.

A logging crew at work in the woods in 1911. By this time, steam power was being used. The large engine at left was known as a donkey engine. It powered gears and winches, which operated the wire ropes that hauled the heavy logs out of the underbrush where they fell. BC Archives E-04615

One important market for British Columbia wood was the Canadian Prairies. After 1900, hundreds of thousands of new immigrants arrived in the Prairie West to homestead farms. The railway connected the Pacific coast across the mountains to this expanding region, where there was a huge demand for lumber.

Above: One of the many steam engines that transported logs out of the woods, along special railways and right to the sawmills. The picture was taken in 1909, near Courtenay on Vancouver Island.
Vancouver Public Library 6044

Left: These sawmill workers, photographed in Vancouver before World War I, were recent immigrants from India. Many newcomers found jobs in sawmills or in logging camps around the province. Vancouver Public Library 7641

FAST FACT
About 55,000 people in BC speak French as their first language.

Union Steamship Company wharf, Vancouver. BC's coastal dwellers relied on the Union Steamship Company to connect them to the outside world.
Gordon Miller painting

Union Steamers

Along the coast of British Columbia, people lived seasonally at canneries and in small fishing and logging camps. There were no roads. Coast dwellers relied on boats to bring in their mail and supplies, take them to other places and keep them in touch with the outside world.

These boats belonged to the fleet of the Union Steamship Company, founded in Vancouver in 1889. Before long its fleet of steamers were cruising the coast all the way north as far as Prince Rupert.

The Union Steamship dock in Vancouver, headquarters of the coastal fleet. Leonard Frank photo, City of Vancouver Archives CVA Wat.P83

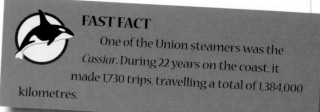

FAST FACT

One of the Union steamers was the *Cassiar*. During 22 years on the coast, it made 1,730 trips, travelling a total of 1,384,000 kilometres.

Union steamers operated on the coast until the 1950s. By then most of the logging camps and fish canneries had closed, and the steamers were replaced by more modern car ferries.

In Their Own Words
BOAT DAY

Boat day, the day the Union steamer arrived, was an exciting time for the people who inhabited these isolated communities. One pioneer wrote:

Old and young live, wait and listen for that ship's shrill whistle. It means our food supplies, mail, familiar faces returning home. On boat days our children are restless at school, coaxing their teacher to let them go down to the wharf to watch the ship come sliding in.

The Lady Alexandra, *pictured here around 1940 at Britannia Beach in Howe Sound, was a well-used member of the Union Steamship fleet. It carried thousands of city dwellers to picnics, dances and excursion spots along the coast.* City of Vancouver Archives CVA 374-182

Coal was King

British Columbia's third important resource industry was mining. Gold was the most important mineral in the early days. It was gold, after all, that had led to the creation of British Columbia. But most of the gold soon disappeared, and coal became the most important mineral in the province.

Coal was like black gold. It was extremely valuable as a fuel to drive the blast furnaces in the factories, the steam engines on the transcontinental railways and other steam machinery of the industrial age. One steady customer for British Columbia coal was the British navy, which used it to fuel their warships patrolling the Pacific.

Nanaimo on Vancouver Island became the centre of coal mining. The town itself sat on a giant coal field, and mineshafts formed a network of underground passages below the town. Some tunnels even ran out under the harbour.

Trouble Underground

Coal mining was very dangerous work. It was not unusual for the walls of tunnels to collapse, trapping the miners underground or burying them alive. Poisonous gases built up in the mines and a stray spark could ignite them

Resources and the Economy

In Their Own Words
BOY MINERS

Boys as young as thirteen years old worked in the coal mines. Usually they worked above ground, looking after the equipment or sorting the coal that came up from below. But many youngsters worked down below as well, eager to earn the higher wages paid to underground workers. One old-timer remembered:

Well, when you were a boy that was all there was around here them days. That's all we had to look forward to.

They couldn't keep me out of the mines. I was bred a coal miner. My father was diggin' coal when he was eleven. He worked in the mines all his life. I left school of my own accord to work in the mines. They wanted me to keep going to school but I said, "No dice!"

I was 15 years old then and like father like son. Anyway, I had a lot of chums that was workin' in the mines and my mother needed the money. The mines was the only thing there was in those days.

From *Boss Whistle*, Lynne Bowen (Oolichan Books, 1982), p. 58.

Young workers at the entrance of the Nanaimo coal mine shaft around 1870. British Columbia Archives C-03710

in deadly explosions. One blast in a Nanaimo mine in 1887 killed 148 miners. Owners, anxious to make profits, did not always take the safety precautions they should.

Workers wanting higher wages and safer working conditions formed unions and went on strike. The longest conflict began in 1912, when Vancouver Island miners walked away from the mines and did not return to work for two years. Mine owners evicted the strikers from their homes and brought in replacement workers to keep the mines open. The government sent in soldiers to prevent violent confrontations between the miners and their replacements. It was one of the worst periods of labour unrest in British Columbia history.

The Kootenay Mining Boom

Coal was not the only mineral mined in British Columbia. Starting in the 1880s, prospectors discovered a series of rich deposits of silver, lead, copper and zinc in the southeast corner of the province, in an area known as the Kootenay.

The Kootenay was a region of high mountains, beautiful lakes and narrow river valleys. It was far from the main cities and difficult to reach. But once rail lines were built and paddlewheel steamboats cruised the lakes, it became possible to start mining the plentiful minerals there.

Some of the richest mines in the world were in the Kootenay. The Sullivan mine at Kimberley was the largest lead-zinc mine in the world. It stayed open until the end of 2001.

Silver was discovered at the Silver King mine near the city of Nelson, and gold at the LeRoi mine at Rossland. More than half of all the copper produced in Canada came from British Columbia. At Trail, the mine owners opened a huge smelter to separate the precious metals from the ore in which they were found. A whole new area of British Columbia was suddenly alive with activity.

A New Economy

Railways connected the coast of British Columbia with the Interior, and BC with markets all over North America. Trains carried timber, minerals and fish across the Rockies, and they returned with grain and other products. Railways spread into isolated parts of the province, making possible new mining and logging ventures.

Once British Columbia had relied for its prosperity on one product at a time: first it was fur, then gold. Now a variety of industries developed. Salmon canneries opened on the coast. Logging camps and sawmills spread through the forests. New mines produced coal and other minerals.

Between 1881 and 1921, the population of British Columbia increased by over ten times. Most of these newcomers got jobs in the new mines, mills, farms and logging camps. The province was no longer a pioneer outpost. It had entered the modern industrial era.

POPULATION OF BC, 1881–1921

1881	49,459
1891	98,173
1901	178,657
1911	392,480
1921	524,582

BC Places
THE LAST STEAMBOAT

Paddlewheel steamboats operated on many of the lakes and rivers of the Interior. On Kootenay Lake, paddlewheelers were active from the 1880s. They were an important link in the transport system that carried supplies and workers to the isolated mines.

The last steamboat to operate in Canada was the SS *Moyie*, which ran on Kootenay Lake from 1898 to 1957. It is the oldest sternwheel paddleboat still in existence anywhere in the world.

The *Moyie* was rescued from oblivion when it retired, and it is berthed on the waterfront in the town of Kaslo. It is an official historic site and visitors are welcome to go on board.

BC Archives I-60959

Students at a traditional one-room school at Eburne, near Vancouver, in 1908. Vancouver Public Library 2134

Workers pose for a photo during the construction of a new post office in Vancouver in 1890. After the railway arrived in Vancouver in 1886, the city grew rapidly. City of Vancouver Archives CVA Bu-P52

GROWTH AND WAR 6

It was a period of rapid economic growth in British Columbia and it was concentrated in the southwest corner of the province, the area that came to be known as the Lower Mainland.

Boom Time

At the beginning of the twentieth century, British Columbia enjoyed a period of rapid expansion. Newcomers poured into the province. Between 1881 and 1921, the population grew from 50,000 to almost 525,000 people.

Most of the newcomers settled in British Columbia's three main cities: New Westminster, Victoria and Vancouver. By the turn of the century, all of these growing communities were equipped with the latest modern conveniences: electric streetcars, electric lights, telephones and fresh drinking water. They were also the main centres of industry in the province.

Children playing on swings in New Westminster, 1902.
Vancouver Public Library Special Collections 2287

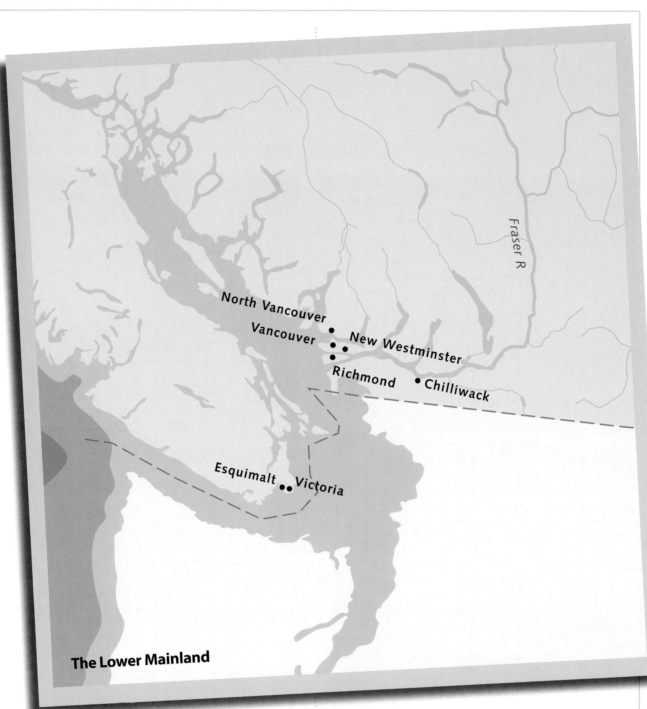

North Vancouver

Vancouver • New Westminster

Richmond
• Chilliwack

Esquimalt •• Victoria

Fraser R

The Lower Mainland

The Royal City

British Columbia's first city was New Westminster, founded in 1859 to be the capital. It is the oldest Canadian city west of Ontario.

New Westminster is located on a hill overlooking the Fraser River not far from its mouth, where an ancient Aboriginal village once stood. The capital of the province moved to Victoria in 1868, but New Westminster continued to grow as an economic centre.

FAST FACT

Originally the community was called Queensborough, after Victoria, Queen of England. The Queen herself preferred New Westminster, so that became the name, but New Westminster has always been known as "the Royal City."

Steamboats travelling on the river stopped there. The salmon-canning industry flourished nearby. Several sawmills were built to make lumber out

POPULATION GROWTH IN BC'S THREE LARGEST CITIES, 1881–1921

	1891	1901	1911	1921
New Westminster	6,678	6,499	13,199	14,495
Victoria	16,841	20,919	31,660	38,727
Vancouver	13,709	27,010	100,401	117,217

of logs from the surrounding forest.

East of New Westminster lay the fertile valley of the Fraser River. As this land filled with settlers growing vegetables and fruit and raising dairy herds, the city became the main market where the farmers brought their produce for sale.

A century ago, cities were built mostly from wood. The buildings were made of lumber, and even the sidewalks were planks. Fire was a constant threat. On the night of September 10, 1898, fire started in a steamboat moored on the waterfront. Flames spread from the boat to a pile of hay stored on the dock. From there the fire swept through the centre of the city, destroying all the buildings in its path. By morning, most of downtown New Westminster lay in ashes.

On September 10, 1898, a fire started in a steamboat and spread quickly through the city, destroying most of downtown New Westminster by morning.

In Their Own Words
THE COLUMBIAN

The local newspaper, *The Columbian*, reported on the blaze:

All up McKenzie, Lorne, Begbie, Alexander and Eighth streets the flames rushed in a mad chase. Thus it was that the whole south side of Columbia Avenue burst into flames practically at the same time. Merchants who had made desperate efforts to save their private papers were drawn from their stores in a rush for life.

The Hotel Douglas became a howling volcano of flame a few minutes after it was first noticed to be on fire. The guests had ample warning though, and all had escaped from the building though few had more of their belongings than what they stood up in.

A sheet of living flame swept across the street and burst in the windows of the splendid Hotel Guichon. The noise was deafening. Above the roar of the flames, repeated explosions could be heard as the fire reached the explosives stored in the warehouses of Columbia and Front streets. The earth trembled with repeated shocks and the crash of breaking glass joined with the jar of falling walls to make the night a horror.

From *The Columbian*, September 17, 1898.

Growth and War

But fire could not destroy the spirit of the residents. Immediately they began rebuilding, with the help of donations that came from across Canada. Within a year, most of downtown New Westminster was rebuilt and the Royal City was back in business.

Electric Streetcars

For many years, travel around the Lower Mainland was by horseback or wagon on dirt roads littered with stumps and boulders. In

FAST FACT
The first electric streetcar in Victoria could reach a speed of 15 kilometres an hour.

A streetcar takes on passengers in Victoria in the 1890s. Note the overhead wires, which carried electricity to the car. The conductor is standing at the control.
BC Archives E-01978

rainy season, the roads turned to mud.

In 1891, an electric railway opened between New Westminster and Vancouver. It was called an interurban railway because it operated between two urban communities. At the time, it was the only interurban in North America. Interurbans ran on steel tracks, just like a steam railway, but they were powered by electricity passing through overhead wires. Each train was connected to the wires by trolley poles.

The Westminster and Vancouver Tramway was just the beginning. Soon electric trains were running between Vancouver and Richmond, and in 1910 a line opened to connect New Westminster to the town of Chilliwack, 100 kilometres away in the Fraser Valley. Farmers used the line to carry their produce to the larger centres. Special trains raced in every day from valley farms, carrying fresh milk for urban households.

Meanwhile, electric streetcars began to operate in the major cities. Victoria was first. In February 1890, Car #1, loaded with dignitaries, rattled down Store Street. It was the official opening of the third street railway in Canada and the first in British Columbia. Four months later, Vancouver opened its street railway, and New Westminster's streetcars began to run the next year.

Street railways had an important effect on the shape of the modern city. They were the first means of moving large numbers of people quickly and cheaply. People no longer had to live close to where they worked. They could live at a distance from their jobs and commute to work by streetcar. Wealthier residents left the inner city and moved to suburbs, away from the hustle and bustle of downtown.

Three women on the sidewalk outside a house in New Westminster in 1902. The woman on the left is Mattie Gunterman, a well-known photographer who was visiting from the Kootenays. Vancouver Public Library Special collections 2413

The Parliament Buildings in Victoria shortly after they opened in 1898. They were designed by Francis Rattenbury, an architect who designed many important public buildings in early British Columbia.

BC Archives E-04093

Capital City

Victoria has had a reputation as a British city for a long time. Many fur traders from the Hudson's Bay Company retired to farm there. In the days of the colony, most government officials came out from England and many stayed on with their families. Their palatial homes were the centre of fashionable society.

Another British influence was the naval base at Esquimalt, next door to Victoria. For many years it was the headquarters of the British navy in the Pacific Ocean. Warships visited the harbour to take on supplies and allow the sailors some time on shore. In 1910 the Canadian navy took over the base, and today

A croquet party at "Fairfield," the Victoria home of Joseph Trutch, an influential government official, around 1870. Garden parties like this one reflected the city's British origins. BC Archives C-05218

Esquimalt remains a naval centre.

The arrival of the railway in Vancouver in 1886 attracted industry to the mainland city. As a result, Victoria took second place as an economic centre. But it was important as the capital of the province. In 1898 the new Parliament Buildings opened. They featured marble walls, stained-glass windows, mahogany carvings and, on the top, a golden statue of Captain George Vancouver. Today the buildings remain the place where the government meets.

BC People
WEST COAST PAINTER

Victoria was home to one of Canada's best artists. She was Emily Carr, born in 1871, the same year that British Columbia entered Confederation. She studied painting in London and Paris, but she found her inspiration in the tall forests and Aboriginal villages of the Pacific coast.

Fearing that the way of life of the First Nations people was disappearing, Carr devoted herself to painting it. She travelled up and down the coast painting totem poles and villages. Often she camped out in the woods by herself.

The house where Carr grew up in Victoria is today a museum open to the public.

In her travels, Emily Carr sometimes camped out in her trailer, which she called the Elephant. In this photograph she is sitting at the door of the Elephant with her monkey, Woo, on her shoulder, and surrounded by pet dogs. BC Archives F-07885

BC Archives D-06009

Growth and War

Asian Newcomers

Among the newcomers pouring into British Columbia were thousands of people from Asia. Many of them were Chinese. They came to work on railway construction, in the salmon canneries and coal mines, and as merchants and farmers.

For the most part, the Chinese newcomers lived together in their own neighbourhoods, called Chinatowns. They wanted to be in familiar surroundings, close to relatives, and

A street in Vancouver's Chinatown in 1904. It is early morning and vegetable farmers have brought their produce to town by wagon to sell. Most Chinese people preferred to live in Chinatown among friends and family. At the same time, in Vancouver the Chinese were not allowed to own property outside Chinatown so they were more or less forced to live there. Vancouver Public Library 6729

THE MIX OF PEOPLE IN BC'S POPULATION IN 1911

British Background	68%
Others from Europe	18%
Asian	8%
Aboriginal	5%
Others	1%

they were not welcome elsewhere. Victoria had the first Chinatown in Canada, and until 1910 it was the largest. Vancouver also attracted many Chinese. Its Chinatown surpassed Victoria's as the largest in Canada and one of the largest in North America.

The Chinese were not the only newcomers from Asia. Immigrants from Japan and India also settled in the city and established their own neighbourhoods.

FAST FACT

In 2006 the government of Canada admitted the head tax was an unjust policy and apologized for it to the Chinese-Canadian community.

By 1911, people from east Asia made up 8 percent of the population of British Columbia. This was not a large number, but it was enough to raise fears among the white majority. Many white British Columbians believed that people from Asia, because of their different customs and languages, would not mix with the rest of society. Workers were afraid that the newcomers would take their jobs. Some white people believed that if Asian immigration continued, the newcomers would soon control British Columbia society.

In response to these fears, the government made laws to restrict immigration to British Columbia from Asia. In 1885 a new tax was

In Their Own Words
A CHINESE HOUSEBOY
Wing Wong, who arrived in Vancouver in 1912 to work as a houseboy, described his life:

I was small in those days, twelve or thirteen. I studied after school and then I did my work: chopping wood, bringing up coal, house cleaning, taking care of the furnace, washing dishes. Just to get my room and board.

Below: *Many young people from China came to British Columbia as servants—houseboys and maids—for white families. This photograph shows a houseboy with his family in Vancouver about 1900.*
BC Archives B-03779

Growth and War

introduced requiring Chinese to pay $50 each to enter Canada. Over the years, this "head tax" rose to $500 (about $4,700 in today's money). No other immigrant group had to pay such a tax. Then, in 1923, the government halted all immigration from China. Other restrictions were put in place against newcomers from India and Japan. At the same time, people of Asian background were not allowed to vote or to hold certain jobs.

The restrictions against Asians remained in force until 1947.

Pacific Port

Few cities have appeared as suddenly as Vancouver. In 1881, a few dozen loggers and sawmill workers lived along the shore of Burrard Inlet. Then the railway arrived, followed by merchants and builders of all descriptions. By

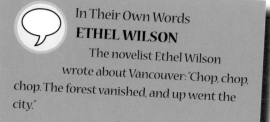

In Their Own Words
ETHEL WILSON
The novelist Ethel Wilson wrote about Vancouver: "Chop, chop, chop. The forest vanished, and up went the city."

1900, the population numbered 27,000 and was growing fast. Where a tall forest had once stood, there were solid stone buildings, paved streets and houses spreading in all directions.

Vancouver faced in two directions at once. It looked outward across the Pacific Ocean to the Orient and Australia, where there was a ready market for its products. Vancouver was a busy port, welcoming ships from around the world. The Canadian Pacific Railway operated a fleet of ocean-going steamships, called the Empress ships, which set a new standard of speed and

History Mystery
WHO MURDERED JANET SMITH?

It is one of the most troubling unsolved murder cases in Vancouver history. On the morning of July 26, 1924, someone shot and killed Janet Smith at her home in the Shaughnessy neighbourhood of Vancouver. Smith was a twenty-two-year-old nanny who came from Scotland to look after the children of a wealthy family. Who would want to harm her?

Police became suspicious of the family's Chinese houseboy, Wong Foon Sing. He was the only other person in the house at the time of the murder. There was no evidence pointing in his direction, but people were prejudiced against him mainly because he was Chinese. At one point police kidnapped Wong and tortured him to get a confession. When he would not confess, Wong was arrested and thrown in jail. But at his trial, the jury let him go for lack of evidence. Angry at the treatment he had received, Wong returned to live in China. Meanwhile, no one ever was convicted of the murder of Janet Smith.

Girl Whose Death Is Being Probed

JANET SMITH, THE Scottish nursemaid in the Baker home on Osler Avenue, as she appeared when photographed a few days before her violent and mysterious death on July 26.

Janet Smith. City of Vancouver Archives

An automobile in Vancouver in the 1920s. Note the wooden plank sidewalk and streets. Only gradually were city streets paved. Vancouver Public Library 7431

elegance. They steamed between Vancouver and the Orient, carrying passengers, mail and cargo of all types. Lumber, salmon, coal and other minerals were shipped to many countries from Vancouver's harbour.

At the same time, Vancouver looked to the Interior. The CPR, and the other railways that followed, connected the port city to the rest of the continent. Goods came by ship to be loaded onto the trains that carried them across the mountains to the Prairies and beyond.

One especially exotic product was silk. It was brought in from China and Japan on the Empress ships, then loaded on trains for shipment to eastern Canada and the United States. Raw silk spoils very quickly, so speed was crucial. When a train carrying silk was passing, all other traffic on the railway stopped.

Vancouver was more than a port city. It was also the centre of industrial activity in the province. The large salmon-canning companies had head offices there. So did the forest industry, which provided more jobs than any other activity. By 1915, three railway lines from across the continent entered the city. Three-quarters of all the goods manufactured in British Columbia were made in Vancouver.

Automobiles began appearing on Vancouver streets in about 1904. The first gasoline car was purchased by John Hendry, a sawmill owner. They rumbled through the streets at 10 kilometres an hour, coughing smoke and frightening horses. For some years, only the wealthy could afford to buy a car. By 1928 there were enough motor cars that a traffic light—the first one in the city—had to be installed on Hastings Street downtown.

One of the CPR's gleaming ships, Empress of Japan, *arriving in Vancouver in 1930.* BC Archives I-60999

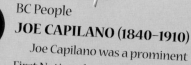

JOE CAPILANO (1840–1910)

Joe Capilano was a prominent First Nations leader, and his wife Mary was a noted storyteller. They were members of the Squamish people, who live in North Vancouver. This photograph shows Joe Capilano in 1906, when he led a group of Aboriginal leaders to London, England. They wanted to explain to the King of England why the Aboriginal people believed they had been pushed off their land by white settlers. But the British government told the delegation that its complaint was a matter for the government of Canada to settle.

North Vancouver Museum 2849

Vancouver's first "skyscraper" was the World Building, so named because it was home to the World newspaper. It was seventeen storeys high. When it was built in 1913, it was the tallest building in the British Empire and a symbol of Vancouver's "big city" status. Vancouver Public Library 4658

World War I

World War I began in 1914 and lasted four years. The fighting occurred far from Canada in Europe, where the armies of Britain, France and Russia struggled against the German and Austrian empires. But many Canadians felt strong ties to Britain and volunteered to join the conflict.

At first the war seemed like a great adventure. Young soldiers hurried to sign up because they feared it would all be over before they could see any action. Only slowly did the true horror of the conflict sink in. Far from ending quickly, the war dragged on year after year. Millions of people died, and millions more soldiers were badly maimed.

After three years of war, Canada began to run short of volunteers willing to fight. In 1917 the government passed a law forcing young men who were not married to join the army. This was called conscription, and it was unpopular with many people who for one reason or another opposed the war.

British Columbia was divided by the impact of war. In some ways the province prospered.

BC People
GINGER GOODWIN
(1887–1918)

One person who refused to fight in the war was Ginger Goodwin. He was a radical labour leader whom the government hoped to send overseas to the battle front. Instead, he hid in the woods near his home on Vancouver Island. A party of police went looking for him and shot him dead. The police said they had acted in self-defence, but to Goodwin's friends, it was murder. A jury set free the officer who had pulled the trigger. Meanwhile, workers staged a huge anti-war protest in Vancouver. Because he was dedicated to the cause of ordinary working people, Goodwin remains a hero to many people.

Shipyards hummed with activity as many battleships and supply vessels were built for the war. The conflict created a huge demand for raw materials produced in British Columbia: copper, lumber, coal and wood.

Vancouver's first airport, shown in 1929. Planes had been used in battle during World War I, but flying as recreation did not catch on until after the war, during the 1920s. These small two-seater aircraft carried sightseers over the city. It was 1939 before the first passenger airplanes began flying from Vancouver to eastern Canada on a regular schedule.

Leonard Frank photo

BC People
PREMIER MCBRIDE

Richard McBride was born in New Westminster and worked as a lawyer before he got into politics.

He became leader of the Conservative Party and was elected premier in 1903. He was thirty-two years old, the youngest person ever to become premier. Voters called him "Handsome Dick," and he was very popular for his friendly, open manner. McBride led his party to victory in four elections. In 1912 he won a knighthood from the King of England, making him the only premier in Canadian history to be called "Sir."

McBride was successful in attracting investors to the province. He made large grants of land to railway, logging and mining companies. His years as premier are sometimes called the "Great Potlatch" because he gave away so many of British Columbia's natural resources.

BC Archives PDP02261

But the cost in human lives was high. BC had more volunteers per capita than any other province in Canada. By war's end, 6,225 British Columbians were dead, and more than 13,000 others suffered horrible wounds.

Women and the War

The outbreak of World War I opened new opportunities for Canadian women. With so many men away in the armed forces, women were called upon to take their place in the work force.

Up to this time, most women had worked mainly in the home, raising children and looking after the household chores. Women with jobs had worked as schoolteachers, nurses or at other traditional jobs. Most of the work world was closed to them.

This changed with the war, and the urgent need for workers in factories and war industries. Women became airplane mechanics and munitions makers. They took jobs in business offices. Some went overseas to serve on the front lines in the medical corps or as ambulance drivers. They also helped out at home, raising money

These women working at a gas station in Vancouver during World War I were part of a whole "army" of women who took over jobs that only men had done before they went to war. Vancouver Public Library Special Collections 13212

and sending food and clothing to the soldiers at the front.

The new importance of women in the work world gave them new influence in the political world as well. Until the war, only men were allowed to vote in elections. That changed in 1917, when British Columbia women won the right to vote in provincial elections. The next year, they were allowed to vote in federal elections as well.

Changes to the law meant that women could run for elected office. In 1918, Mary Ellen Smith of Vancouver became the first woman anywhere in Canada to be elected to a provincial parliament. A few years later she became a cabinet minister in the BC government—another first.

The right to vote was not won by all women, however. First Nations women and women of Asian background were still denied the vote, along with their menfolk.

Killer Epidemic

With the end of war came a new killer. An outbreak of deadly influenza began in Europe and was carried to Canada by soldiers coming home from war. Before it was over, the flu killed 21 million people worldwide, 50,000 in Canada.

The first cases appeared in British Columbia in October 1918. People caught it from each other easily, so health officials asked everyone to avoid public places where they might be infected. Schools, shops, churches and theatres

Mary Ellen Smith was a Vancouver politician. In 1918 she became the first woman elected to a provincial parliament. BC Archives B-01563

all closed. Public meetings of all kinds were banned. Hospitals filled to overflowing. People wore masks over their faces to keep from spreading germs. Doctors were powerless. There was no drug or vaccine for the flu—patients could only stay in bed and hope to get better.

By the time the epidemic faded away in the spring of 1919, about one out of every three people had been sick. In Vancouver alone, 900 people died. It was the worst public health disaster since the smallpox epidemic many years earlier.

The New City

Industry and immigration together created a new kind of city. New Westminster, Vancouver and Victoria were very unlike the small farming and trading communities of British Columbia's early years. They were bigger, noisier, richer and more varied.

The new city was divided into neighbourhoods of rich and poor. Immigrants from China, Japan and India lived in their own neighbourhoods. For some people, the city presented great opportunities. For others, it brought poverty and injustice.

One of the biggest changes was the rapid growth of the Lower Mainland. When British Columbia joined Confederation in 1871, not many people lived in that part of the province. Then, with the arrival of the railway, the Lower Mainland boomed. By the 1920s, Vancouver and its surrounding area was home to about half of all the people who lived in BC, and its industries were producing most of the wealth.

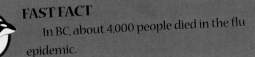

FAST FACT
In BC, about 4,000 people died in the flu epidemic.

Unemployed men climbing aboard the protest train at Kamloops in 1935, on their way to Ottawa to meet the prime minister. National Archives C-029399

HARD TIMES AND WAR

Hard times came to British Columbia during the 1930s. The Great Depression brought unemployment, poverty and business collapse. It was not until the outbreak of World War II that the economy improved. Then war brought suffering of a different kind.

The Great Depression

For most British Columbians, the 1920s was a prosperous decade. Jobs were plentiful, industry thrived and the province grew rapidly.

The good times came to an end, however, with an abrupt crash. In October 1929, the stock exchange in New York City collapsed, and echoes were heard around the world. Businesses went bankrupt. People lost their life savings. At the same time, the prices of natural resources—lumber, minerals, and grain—began to fall. Canada, and particularly British Columbia, could not rely on the sale of its resources to support the economy.

Factories, mines and logging camps closed, and workers lost their jobs. By 1933, almost one out of every three workers in Canada was unemployed. Those lucky enough to remain at work were paid less money. Poverty and hardship were widespread. It was a time known as the Great Depression.

Living in the Jungle

When they were unable to find jobs where they lived, many young men and women left home to seek work elsewhere. Without any money, they could not afford to pay for train tickets, food or hotel rooms. Instead they sneaked aboard freight trains and rode for free. This was called "riding the rails."

FAST FACT
By 1931, BC had the highest level of unemployment of any province in Canada—27 percent of workers did not have a job.

Faces of the Depression: three unemployed men in Vancouver, 1931. During the hard times of the 1930s, many Canadian men and women lost their jobs and their savings. City of Vancouver Archives Re N8.2

When they came to a town, they went from door to door and begged for food. They slept outside in camps of unemployed people known as "jungles." "In every town there was a 'jungle' where no one bothered you," recalled one man who lived this life for several years. "This is where I cooked my meals over a jungle fire and had a short nap while waiting for the next freight train out."

Wandering unemployed people tended to gather in cities, where they hoped work might be available. The police worried that so many strangers might cause trouble. City officials did not want to pay for taking care of them. As a result, the jobless were often hassled and hurried on their way.

On the Relief

So many people were unemployed that the government had to do something. Public assistance was a new idea in Canada in the 1930s. Unlike today, there was no social

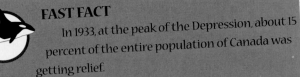

One of the "Jungles" where unemployed people lived in the 1930s. The man in the suit on the left is Reverend Andrew Roddan, a church minister who tried to help people in Vancouver who had lost their jobs.
City of Vancouver Archives Re N4.1

In Their Own Words
A WORKER

A worker from Vancouver Island wrote to Canadian Prime Minister R.B. Bennett about the Depression:

Please pardon me for writing you, but I am in such a circumstance that I really do not know what to do. When will this distress amongst the people come to an end and how long will this starvation last? I am on the relief and only get 4 days work on the public roads. That is not enough for both of us to live on. Next came my land taxes. If I don't pay it this year, then the government of BC will have my 40 acres and I and my wife will be on the bare ground. Is that the way the Government will help the poor men?

From *The Wretched of Canada: Letters to R.B. Bennett, 1930–1935,* L.M. Grayson and Michael Bliss (University of Toronto, 1971), p.160.

welfare, no employment insurance, nothing at all to help people who could not find work and had spent or lost their savings.

Faced with a crisis, the government began a system of relief. When people became penniless, they could apply for assistance. It did not amount to much, but for thousands of families it was better than nothing.

Another response by the government was to set up work camps for single men. The camps were located away from the cities. The men who stayed there received meals, a bed and 20 cents a day (about $3 in today's money) in return for working on road-building and logging projects. There were more than 200 camps across British

Columbia. No one was forced to go to them, but for many men it was the only way to get food and shelter.

Rum Running

One job that was always available for the adventurous was rum running. Between 1920 and 1933, during a period called Prohibition, it was illegal to sell or produce liquor in the

Hard Times and War

United States. Americans who wanted a drink of liquor had to smuggle it into the country from outside—which is where the rum runners came in.

Rum runners were smugglers from British Columbia who carried liquor down the coast into the United States. In the dead of night they raced their speedy boats across Juan de Fuca Strait to hidden harbours in Washington State.

Vancouver police are racing to the scene of a protest by unemployed workers at the city's post office in June 1938. It was one of several protests in the city during the Great Depression of the 1930s. The tanker truck in the background was used to clean the streets. Vancouver Public Library 1294

There the cargo was picked up by trucks and carried to customers in the city. Sometimes large freighters loaded with cases of liquor anchored far offshore, where the American Coast Guard was not authorized to arrest them. Smaller boats rushed back and forth between the freighters on "Rum Row" and the shore, delivering their illegal freight.

The liquor traffic produced large profits and soon attracted big-time criminals. Rum runners fought with one another for control of the business. The Coast Guard did its best to chase down the boats and arrest the smugglers. It was a bit like the Wild West at sea, and rum runners had to be people who liked danger and adventure.

When finally the American government ended Prohibition in 1933, there was no longer a need for smuggling and the rum-running era ended.

Protest

As the Depression grew worse, unemployed people began to grow angry. They demanded solutions to their problems. They resented being cooped up in relief camps, which they said were no better than jails. They did not like being treated like criminals when their only "crime" was being out of work in an economy that did not have enough jobs for everyone.

In April 1935, an army of unemployed men left the Interior camps and marched down to Vancouver, demanding "work and wages." From Vancouver the protestors set out riding the rails across Canada. They planned to carry their demands to the prime minister in Ottawa, and so the protest was called the On-to-Ottawa Trek.

As the train rolled through British Columbia and the Prairies, it picked up more protestors along the way. In Regina, the capital city of Saskatchewan, police ordered the train to halt, and a small delegation of protestors went ahead to Ottawa to talk with Prime Minister Bennett. Bennett was not sympathetic. He sent the delegation away empty-handed.

Back in Regina, the protest turned violent. At a huge outdoor rally, police charged the crowd, swinging clubs and making arrests. One police officer was killed and many protestors were injured. The so-called Regina Riot brought an end to the On-to-Ottawa protest.

Bloody Sunday

There was no end in sight for the Depression, and in April 1938, the government closed its work camps. Men who were unemployed and not married were not eligible to receive relief. The government did offer to pay for these men

FAST FACT
Bloody Sunday, as it was called, ended with thousands of dollars' worth of damage, hundreds of people injured and 22 protestors in jail.

to travel to other provinces to look for work. But there *was* no work. A group of protestors gathered in Vancouver to press the government to act.

On May 20, about 1,200 men entered the city post office, the art gallery and a downtown hotel. They sat down on the floor and refused to move until the government did something. Such a large number of people could not be arrested. It would fill the jails to overflowing. Instead, officials decided to wait and see what happened.

At last the police lost patience. Early on the morning of June 19, RCMP and city police moved in to evict the sit-downers. Some men left peacefully, having made their point. At the post office, however, police used tear gas and clubs to drive protestors into the street. Hundreds of people were injured. Furious at the police, a crowd marched through downtown Vancouver, breaking store windows.

At a huge outdoor rally in a downtown park, unemployed people and their supporters condemned police violence. "We want something done for these people," one speaker declared, referring to the unemployed. The government responded with emergency relief, and tempers cooled.

Fishing Strike

Not all protest during the Depression was violent. Many workers staged peaceful strikes to try to improve their wages and working conditions. One of the most important strikes in British Columbia during the 1930s was the fishing strike of 1938.

Fishers sold their catch each summer to the

Hard Times and War

BC People
AT HOME ON A BOAT

Most children in British Columbia lived in the cities, but one family spent their time cruising the coast in a small (7.6 metres) boat called the *Caprice*. The five Blanchet (*blon-SHET*) children—Frances, Peter, Betty, David and Joan—lived on the boat with their mother, who was called Capi because she was the captain.

Every summer in the 1930s, the Blanchets left their house in town to roam the inlets and islands of the coast, looking for new things to see and do. They were especially interested in visiting the village sites of the Aboriginal people, where totem poles and cedar houses stood silently in the forest.

The boat was not large, but somehow they found space for everyone. At night, when they tied up to shore, the family dog warned them if a wandering cougar or bear got too close.

Later in her life, Capi Blanchet wrote a book, *The Curve of Time*, about life aboard her boat. It is a wonderful story about a footloose family and its adventures among the people and animals of the coast.

The Blanchets on one of their summer excursions in the 1930s. From left to right, Frances, Peter, Betty, David, Joan and Capi. Raincoast Chronicles Six/Ten (Harbour, 1983)

Members of the 1938 strike committee. A Ripple, A Wave, (Fisherman Publishing Society, 1974)

canneries all along the coast. The owners of the canneries were used to paying whatever they wanted for the fish. In 1938, the owners suddenly reduced the price they paid for salmon. This time the fishers did not accept. Instead, they tied up their boats and refused to produce any fish.

It was a bitter strike. In many small fishing communities, the only store was owned by the canning company and these were closed to strikers. Owners brought in other fishers to try to keep a supply of fish coming into the canneries. At the height of the strike, dozens of boats got together and travelled down the coast to Vancouver, where they entered the harbour in two long lines. This defiant action carried the protest right to the heart of British Columbia's largest city.

As more and more fishers joined the strike and tied up their boats, the canners had to give in. An agreement was reached that gave fishers a better price for their salmon. It was the first time that fishers on the Pacific coast had acted together to challenge the power of the owners.

A New Party

During the Depression, people all across the country decided that the political system needed a change. They believed that the old system could not provide for people in times of economic crisis. Some of these people took part in protests like the one in Vancouver. Others decided to form new political parties.

In 1933, a group of workers, farmers and reformers got together in Regina, Saskatchewan, to create a new party. They called themselves the Co-operative Commonwealth Federation, or CCF for short.

The CCF wanted a much larger role for government in the lives of Canadians. It blamed banks and large corporations for the Depression. CCFers wanted to make sure that all Canadians, rich and poor alike, had jobs, education and health care.

The CCF had a lot of support in British Columbia. It became the second most popular party with voters. In 1961 the CCF changed its name to the New Democratic Party. It is still active in politics today.

Creating the Welfare State

Eventually the worst of the economic crisis passed, but no one who lived through the Depression would ever forget the hard times. Canadians were determined that never again would so many people suffer so much hardship.

The Depression changed many people's minds about the role of government in society. People realized that they and their neighbours could lose their livelihood through no fault of their own. Canadians came to accept that government had a role to play helping people when times were bad. This was one of the ideas

BC People
GRACE MACINNIS (1905–1991)

Grace MacInnis was an early worker for the CCF in BC. Her father, J.S. Woodsworth, was the new party's first leader, and her husband, Angus MacInnis, was a CCF Member of Parliament from Vancouver.

MacInnis herself decided to run for election. In 1941 she became a member of the BC Legislature, one of fourteen CCF candidates who won seats that year. Both in and out of the legislature, she continued to be an active leader of the party.

When Angus died in 1964, she decided to run for a seat in the federal Parliament. By this time the CCF had become the New Democratic Party (NDP). MacInnis won a Vancouver riding for the NDP, becoming the first British Columbia woman elected to Parliament. She kept her seat until 1974, when poor health forced her to quit politics.

The Lions Gate Bridge is a Vancouver landmark. It connects the downtown part of the city through Stanley Park to the North Shore mountains. It was built during the Depression, partly to give jobs to unemployed workers. Vancouver Public Library Special Collections 12320

that made the CCF popular with voters.

In the years that followed, a number of government programs were created to help the poor, the sick and the jobless. Taken together, these programs are what is known as the welfare state. They include health care insurance, pension plans and schemes to help the unemployed. The purpose of the welfare state was to create a safety net so that no one could lose everything they had because of sickness or job loss.

World War, Again

In 1939, world war broke out. Once again, the battleground was Europe, where Germany and Italy, known as the Axis, fought against Great Britain, France and their allies. And once again, Canadians volunteered by the thousands to fight for the Allies.

War went a long way toward relieving the country's economic problems. The number of unemployed people dropped as men and women hurried to join the armed forces. The demand for war goods grew. Industries geared

BC People
DUFF PATTULLO

In the middle of the Depression, British Columbia voters went to the polls. They voted out the old government, which they blamed for not doing anything about the economic crisis, and they turned to Duff Pattullo, leader of the Liberal Party.

Pattullo was a politician from Prince Rupert. He came to office with new ideas for coping with the Depression. He thought that the government should play a larger role in the economy, especially to help the poorest members of society. He put unemployed people to work building roads and bridges, and he began a system of medical insurance.

Pattullo was disappointed that the federal government in Ottawa would not give him enough money to do even more to boost the economy. He called himself "a British Columbian Canadian," meaning that he put the needs of his province first. "We are an empire in ourselves," he said, "and our hills and valleys are stored with potential wealth." He spent much of his time as premier quarrelling with the government in Ottawa.

Pattullo remained premier until 1941. The Pattullo Bridge over the Fraser River is named for him.

Premier Duff Pattullo talks with a future voter in 1941. Pattullo was premier of British Columbia from 1933 to 1941. City of Vancouver Archives PORT- P.817

These women worked as welders in a shipyard in Victoria during World War II. BC Archives 95128

Hard Times and War

A young boy says goodbye to his father, who is marching through the streets of New Westminster on his way to war in 1940. Claude P. Dettloff photo, National Archives C38723

up to produce ships, airplanes, munitions, building materials and many other items.

Once again, women stepped into the jobs left by their brothers and husbands who had gone to war. They went to work in war industries, on the farm and on construction projects. In peacetime, this kind of work was considered unsuitable for women. In wartime, they kept the economy going.

More than that, women were accepted into the Canadian armed forces for the first time. The army created the Canadian Women's Army Corps, followed by the navy and air force.

People on the coast were so worried about an invasion that children in school practised wearing gas masks in case of an enemy attack. Vancouver Public Library Special Collections 44965

FAST FACT
By 1945, more than 43,000 Canadian women had joined the armed forces.

The Home Front

The war caused shortages in the everyday life of Canadians. Products such as rubber, gasoline, iron and many food items were much in demand for use in the war. Back at home, consumers had to go without.

In 1941, rationing became a fact of life for Canadians. Every person received a ration book. It contained a number of coupons that could be used to obtain coffee, milk, sugar, butter and other basic food items. Gasoline, which was so vital for the war, was also rationed, along with

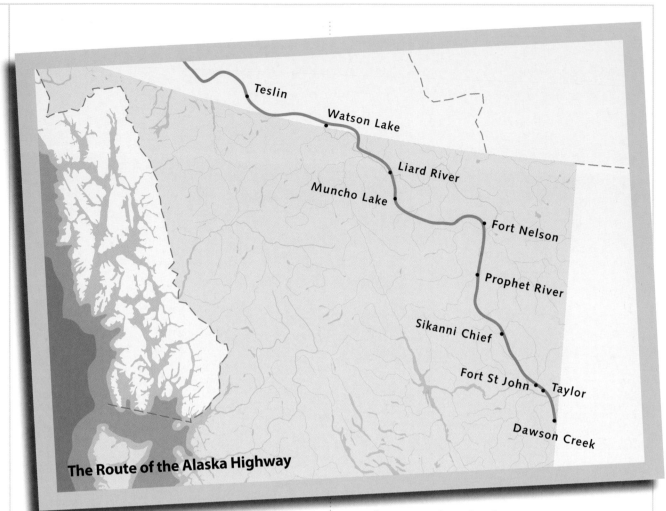

The Route of the Alaska Highway

rubber tires. Many people just stopped driving for as long as the war continued.

No one was allowed to waste anything. People tried to grow as much of their own food as they could. Children went door to door collecting scrap metal that might be used for making military equipment. The war was an all-out effort.

War in the North

On December 7, 1941, Japan launched a surprise attack on Pearl Harbor, an American naval base in Hawaii. Canada, along with the United States, immediately declared war on Japan. It was truly a world war now.

The Americans worried that Japan might invade North America through Alaska. In order to get troops and supplies to the North, the Americans decided to build a highway across northern British Columbia.

The Alaska Highway, as it came to be called, ran from Dawson Creek to Watson Lake in the Yukon. It was built very quickly by thousands of American soldiers. After the war it was taken over by Canada. Today the Alaska Highway is still an important route through northern British Columbia.

The Gumboot Navy

When World War II began, Canada's navy was concentrated on the Atlantic coast, and the coast of British Columbia was defenceless against attack or invasion. What the coast did have was a lot of fishers, and no one knew the waters and the coastline better. The government decided to transform the fishing fleet into a navy.

Officially they were the Fishermen's Reserve, but everyone knew them as the Gumboot Navy.

The Nenamook *was one of the fish boats in the Gumboot Navy during World War II.* BC Archives 89416

In total, there were 42 fish boats and 975 fishers. They were given guns and sent out in all kinds of weather to look for enemy submarines.

After the attack on Pearl Harbor, people in British Columbia had a real fear of an invasion by Japan. While the invasion never came, the Gumboot Navy took seriously its role as the first line of defence. By 1944, as the threat of invasion eased, the force had disbanded and the crews had gone back to fishing.

Treatment of the Japanese

Japanese people were never completely welcome in British Columbia. Strict limits were set on the number of people who were allowed to enter from Japan. Like other Asian newcomers and Aboriginal people, they were not allowed to vote or to hold certain jobs.

When war began, this animosity deepened. Many British Columbians wondered how

In Their Own Words
WE WERE GOOD CANADIANS

Joy Kogawa was a young girl who was removed from Vancouver with her family and sent to live in the Interior. Many years later she wrote about her experience:

It is hard to understand, but Japanese Canadians were treated as enemies at home, even though we were good Canadians. Not one Japanese Canadian was ever found to be traitor to our country. Yet our cameras and cars, radios and fishing boats were taken away. After that our homes and businesses and farms were also taken and we were sent to live in camps in the mountains. Fathers and older brothers and uncles were made to work building roads in the Rocky Mountains. If you ever drive through these beautiful mountains, you may ride over some roads made by Japanese Canadians.

From *Naomi's Road,* Joy Kogawa (Toronto: Oxford University Press, 1986).

Above: From 1914 to 1941, the Asahi (a Japanese word meaning "morning sun") was one of the best baseball teams in Vancouver. It was the pride of the Japanese community. All the best players wanted to belong. The team disbanded when most of the players were sent away from the coast during World War II. Sanmiya Family Collection. Japanese Canadian National Museum 94/41.018

NOTICE

TO ALL PERSONS OF JAPANESE RACIAL ORIGIN

Having reference to the Protected Area of British Columbia as described in an Extra of the Canada Gazette, No. 174 dated Ottawa, Monday, February 2, 1942:-

1. EVERY PERSON OF THE JAPANESE RACE, WHILE WITHIN THE PROTECTED AREA AFORESAID, SHALL HEREAFTER BE AT HIS USUAL PLACE OF RESIDENCE EACH DAY BEFORE SUNSET AND SHALL REMAIN THEREIN UNTIL SUNRISE ON THE FOLLOWING DAY, AND NO SUCH PERSON SHALL GO OUT OF HIS USUAL PLACE OF RESIDENCE AFORESAID UPON THE STREETS OR OTHERWISE DURING THE HOURS BETWEEN SUNSET AND SUNRISE;

2. NO PERSON OF THE JAPANESE RACE SHALL HAVE IN HIS POSSESSION OR USE IN SUCH PROTECTED AREA ANY MOTOR VEHICLE, CAMERA, RADIO TRANSMITTER, RADIO RECEIVING SET, FIREARM, AMMUNITION OR EXPLOSIVE;

3. IT SHALL BE THE DUTY OF EVERY PERSON OF THE JAPANESE RACE HAVING IN HIS POSSESSION OR UPON HIS PREMISES ANY ARTICLE MENTIONED IN THE NEXT PRECEDING PARAGRAPH, FORTHWITH TO CAUSE SUCH ARTICLE TO BE DELIVERED UP TO ANY JUSTICE OF THE PEACE RESIDING IN OR NEAR THE LOCALITY WHERE ANY SUCH ARTICLE IS HAD IN POSSESSION, OR TO AN OFFICER OR CONSTABLE OF THE POLICE FORCE OF THE PROVINCE OR CITY IN OR NEAR SUCH LOCALITY OR TO AN OFFICER OR CONSTABLE OF THE ROYAL CANADIAN MOUNTED POLICE.

4. ANY JUSTICE OF THE PEACE OR OFFICER OR CONSTABLE RECEIVING ANY ARTICLE MENTIONED IN PARAGRAPH 2 OF THIS ORDER SHALL GIVE TO THE PERSON DELIVERING THE SAME A RECEIPT THEREFOR AND SHALL REPORT THE FACT TO THE COMMISSIONER OF THE ROYAL CANADIAN MOUNTED POLICE, AND SHALL RETAIN OR OTHERWISE DISPOSE OF ANY SUCH ARTICLE AS DIRECTED BY THE SAID COMMISSIONER.

5. ANY PEACE OFFICER OR ANY OFFICER OR CONSTABLE OF THE ROYAL CANADIAN MOUNTED POLICE HAVING POWER TO ACT AS SUCH PEACE OFFICER OR OFFICER OR CONSTABLE IN THE SAID PROTECTED AREA, IS AUTHORIZED TO SEARCH WITHOUT WARRANT THE PREMISES OR ANY PLACE OCCUPIED OR BELIEVED TO BE OCCUPIED BY ANY PERSON OF THE JAPANESE RACE REASONABLY SUSPECTED OF HAVING IN HIS POSSESSION OR UPON HIS PREMISES ANY ARTICLE MENTIONED IN PARAGRAPH 2 OF THIS ORDER, AND TO SEIZE ANY SUCH ARTICLE FOUND ON SUCH PREMISES;

6. EVERY PERSON OF THE JAPANESE RACE SHALL LEAVE THE PROTECTED AREA AFORESAID FORTHWITH;

7. NO PERSON OF THE JAPANESE RACE SHALL ENTER SUCH PROTECTED AREA EXCEPT UNDER PERMIT ISSUED BY THE ROYAL CANADIAN MOUNTED POLICE;

8. IN THIS ORDER "PERSONS OF THE JAPANESE RACE" MEANS, AS WELL AS ANY PERSON WHOLLY OF THE JAPANESE RACE, A PERSON NOT WHOLLY OF THE JAPANESE RACE IF HIS FATHER OR MOTHER IS OF THE JAPANESE RACE AND IF THE COMMISSIONER OF THE ROYAL CANADIAN MOUNTED POLICE BY NOTICE IN WRITING HAS REQUIRED OR REQUIRES HIM TO REGISTER PURSUANT TO ORDER-IN-COUNCIL P.C. 9760 OF DECEMBER 16th, 1941.

DATED AT OTTAWA THIS 26th DAY OF FEBRUARY, 1942.

Louis S. St. Laurent,
Minister of Justice

To be posted in a Conspicuous Place

Left: Posters like this one were put up in all coastal areas of BC in 1942. They warned Japanese Canadians that they were not allowed to remain on the coast.

Japanese Canadians would behave now that Canada was at war with Japan. There was a great fear on the Coast that Japanese warships might invade across the Pacific. If that happened, would the Japanese living in British Columbia be loyal to their new home, or their old?

About 23,000 people of Japanese background were living in British Columbia when the war began. Most of these people were citizens of Canada, and many had been born in BC. They considered Canada their home. So they were shocked early in 1942 when the government announced that all people of Japanese background living along the coast of British Columbia had to move away.

Over the next few months, about twenty thousand people were forced from their homes. They were loaded on trains and sent to live in camps in the Interior of the province. Some were sent to the Prairies and Ontario. They were treated like prisoners and not allowed to move around without written permission. Once they were gone, the government sold their possessions.

As it turned out, Japan did not invade. Japanese Canadians were allowed to return to the Pacific coast after the war, and prejudice against them slowly ebbed away. In 1949 they received the right to vote, like every other citizen.

Finally, in 1988, the federal government admitted that the treatment of Japanese Canadians during World War II had been unjust. It apologized and agreed to pay compensation to every person who had had to move during the war. It also set up a fund to support educational and cultural projects by the Japanese Canadian community.

The War Is Over

On August 14, 1945, Canadians celebrated the end of war. In every city and town across the country, people poured into the streets, honked their car horns and threw paper streamers into the air. After six long years of war, it was the beginning of peace.

The previous fifteen years had been hard ones. First there was the economic crisis of the Great Depression, when so many people lost their jobs, their homes and their life savings. Then there was the war, when everything—including loved ones—had to be sacrificed to ensure victory.

As they celebrated a return to peace, British Columbians hoped for a return to prosperity as well. After so much turmoil and suffering, they just wanted life to be normal again.

John Landy and Roger Bannister at the British Empire Games in Vancouver, 1954. *British Columbia Sports Hall of Fame*

John Landy
3:59.6

Roger Bannister
3:58·8

BOOM TIMES 8

With the end of World War II, British Columbia entered a period of economic expansion. A new railway reached into the North. New mines, highways, dams and mills were built. At the same time, many of the barriers that once divided different groups began to come down. First Nations people and newcomers from Asia and other parts of the world took on greater roles in society.

Time for a Change

At the end of World War II, British Columbians decided it was time for a change. During the war, the two major political parties—the Liberals and the Conservatives—had formed a coalition. They had run the government together for many years. With the emergency of war over, the partners began to squabble. At the same time, a new force emerged on the political scene.

Social Credit

The new force was called Social Credit.

BC Spotlight

THE MIRACLE MILE

The photograph at the start of this chapter shows the finish of the "Miracle Mile" at the British Empire Games in Vancouver in 1954. It was a "miracle" because for the first time two athletes ran a mile in under 4 minutes in the same race. The photograph shows Roger Bannister of Britain crossing the finish line less than one second ahead of Australia's John Landy. It was the first international sporting event shown live on television across North America. And it was the lead article in the first issue of *Sports Illustrated* magazine. Often forgotten is another runner, BC's own Bill Parnell, who held the mile record for the Empire Games before Bannister and Landy broke it.

Post-war British Columbia

It was a new political party, formed early in the 1950s. Its leader was W.A.C. Bennett, a hardware store owner from Kelowna. In the 1952 election, Social Credit won one more seat than the CCF and formed a new government. W.A.C. Bennett became premier, a job he held for the next twenty years, longer than anyone else in BC history.

Bennett was a born salesperson. He was full of energy and loved to give long speeches.

More than that, he liked to get things done. His rivals called him "Wacky," but "Wily" would have been a better nickname. He was a clever politician who seemed to understand exactly what the voters wanted.

Bennett's government embarked on a massive building program. New highways spread through the Interior. New bridges spanned the rivers. Social Credit opened the University of Victoria and Simon Fraser University in Burnaby, built a railway to the North and created a fleet

It is often said that BC has the largest navy in the world. This "navy" is actually a fleet of ferries that connect many places on the coast. BC Ferries operates forty vessels and handles 22 million passengers a year.
BC Ferries

of coastal ferries. At times it seemed as if the whole province was under construction.

Dam Builder

Premier Bennett needed a way to pay for all this development. He believed he had found the way with the construction of large hydroelectric dams. Hydroelectricity is electricity produced by the force of water. A dam blocks the flow of water in a river to create a large lake, or reservoir. As the water flows out of the reservoir, it is transformed into electrical energy by a giant machine called a turbine. The electricity that is produced is used in homes and as a fuel for industry.

In 1961, Bennett took over a private electrical company and created BC Hydro, a government agency. BC Hydro went to work building huge dams on the Columbia River in the south and the Peace River in the north. Vast areas of land were flooded to create reservoirs behind the dams. One of the dams, named for Premier Bennett, created Williston Lake, the largest lake

in BC. The underground powerhouse was the largest in the world when it opened in 1968. Another, the Mica Dam, stands as tall as an eighty-storey building. The electricity produced by these dams fuelled the growth of British Columbia. Whatever was left over was sold in the United States.

The Little Railway That Grew

Another Social Credit project was British Columbia's own railway, the Pacific Great Eastern (PGE). The other railways ran east–west across the province. The idea of the PGE was to connect the south coast with the northern Interior. Construction on the railway began long before Premier Bennett came to power. But work went slowly, and the line went bankrupt

The Route of the Pacific Great Eastern Railway

The Pacific Great Eastern railway was built in stages. Eventually it reached from North Vancouver all the way to the Peace River Country and had more than 2,000 kilometres of track.

after just a few kilometres of track had been laid.

People made fun of the little railway that seemed to go from nowhere to nowhere. They called it the Please Go Easy, or the Prince George Eventually. The government took control of the line, but still not much work was done.

Premier Bennett's government realized how important the railway could be and finally completed the work. The railway ran from North Vancouver all the way to Fort St. John and Fort Nelson, two towns in the far northeast

corner of the province. By 1971, the remote North had its first rail connection to the coast. Coal, wheat and other products began flowing south by train. The railway played an important part in tying together the different parts of the province.

Resource Towns

The end of the war brought a great demand for British Columbia's resources. Minerals and timber were needed to build homes and fuel factories across Canada and around the world.

Many of the mines and logging camps were located in remote parts of the province, far from the main cities. Companies created instant

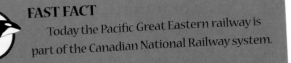

FAST FACT
Today the Pacific Great Eastern railway is part of the Canadian National Railway system.

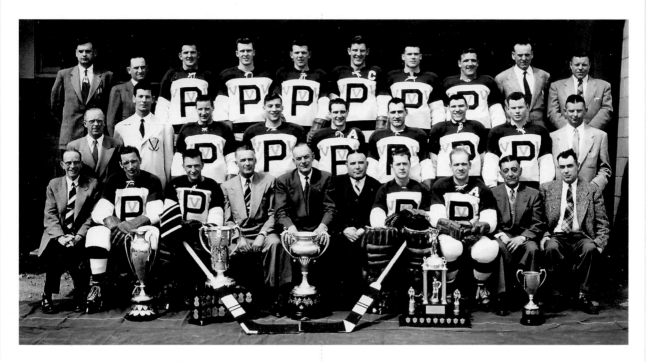

During the 1950s, Canada produced the best hockey teams in the world. Teams from the NHL did not compete at world championships, so the way was open for small-town teams with part-time players. One of these teams was the Penticton Vees. In 1955, this fruit-growing town in the Okanagan Valley sent a team to the world championships in Moscow—and came home with the winner's trophy. BC Sports Hall of Fame

towns for their workers to live in.

One such town was Kitimat. Early in the 1950s the Aluminum Company of Canada (Alcan) began to build a smelter at the head of Douglas Channel far up the north coast. An aluminum smelter is a large plant where ore called bauxite is melted down to produce aluminum metal. This process requires a lot of electrical power, and there was a good source of power near the Douglas Channel site. Alcan called the smelter, and the town it built to house the workers, Kitimat, for the local First Nations people.

Bauxite was brought to Kitimat by freighter from mines in Jamaica, Guyana and Australia. After processing, the refined aluminum was shipped to customers around the world. Today about eleven thousand people live in Kitimat, and most of them work for the Alcan smelter.

Another resource town on the north coast was Ocean Falls. It was the site of a large pulp and paper mill that was powered by electricity produced from a waterfall nearby.

Ocean Falls was the rainiest community in Canada. It was known for producing world-class swimmers, as well as pulp and paper. At its peak, the population was about four thousand people. Then the mill closed. Without work, people had to move away. Today hardly anyone lives where Ocean Falls used to be.

BC People
BRUCE HUTTON

The indoor swimming pool at Ocean Falls opened in 1928 and produced some of the finest swimmers in Canada for several decades. Among the best was Bruce Hutton. During his career, which lasted from 1963 to 1972, he won twenty-four international swimming medals and held eleven Canadian fastest times. In 1968 he held the world record for the freestyle event and won a silver medal at the Olympics. After he retired from swimming, Hutton became a Vancouver police officer.

People in BC began to get television sets in their homes in the early 1950s. This is one of the earliest models, with a small circular screen. At first viewers in Vancouver and Victoria could pick up stations beaming programs across the border from the United States. Then, in 1953, the CBC launched BC's first television station, CBUT in Vancouver. CBUT presented made-in-Canada programs for local audiences. BC Archives 1-02030

Not all instant towns were on the coast. Mackenzie (population 6,000) is located in the Interior, close to the Rocky Mountains. It was created in 1966 when logging companies began operations in the surrounding forests. Mackenzie has two pulp mills, a mill that produces newsprint (the kind of paper that newspapers are printed on) and several sawmills. It is named for the explorer Alexander Mackenzie.

The Northeast

The northeast corner of British Columbia is especially rich in natural resources. During the 1950s, large amounts of oil and natural gas were discovered in this area. These two fuels run the machinery of industry, produce heat for our homes and drive our cars. Oil and gas are both found in pools deep under the ground. Crews dig wells to tap into these pools and bring the oil and gas to the surface. Then it is carried in pipelines to the large cities where it is needed.

Fort St. John is the centre of this industry. It is located on the Alaska Highway and calls itself the Energy Capital of BC. The Peace River flows eastward through this corner of the province into Alberta, so it is often called the Peace River Country.

Coal is another valuable resource that comes from the northeast. The town of Tumbler Ridge sprang to life in 1981 to provide homes for mining families from two huge coal mines that opened nearby. Much of the coal that was mined at Tumbler Ridge was sold in Japan.

BC People
NANCY GREENE

Nancy Greene grew up in Rossland, one of the resource towns of the Interior. She began skiing as a youngster on nearby Red Mountain.

When Greene was seventeen years old she joined Canada's national ski team and began racing in competitions in Europe and the United States. By 1967 she was one of the best skiers in the world. At the 1968 Olympics she won a gold medal in the giant slalom race and a silver medal in the slalom. No wonder she was named Canada's Athlete of the Year.

Today, Nancy Greene and her husband manage a ski resort near Kamloops, BC.

A Society of Many Cultures

Following World War II, the Japanese Canadians who had been sent away from the coast were allowed to return. British Columbians came to realize that they had to become more open to people of different cultural backgrounds.

In 1947, people of Asian heritage were allowed to vote in elections. Then, in the 1960s, restrictions on the number of immigrants from Asian countries allowed into Canada began to be relaxed. Since that time, British Columbia's population has become much more diverse as

Nancy Greene, centre, won a gold and a silver medal at the 1968 Grenoble Winter Olympics. BC Sports Hall of Fame

A group of Doukhobors in British Columbia around 1910. BC Archives A-02072

people have come to live here from many parts of the world. This is what is meant when BC is described as a multicultural society.

One sign of changing attitudes was the arrival of the "boat people" in the 1970s. They were Chinese and Vietnamese refugees who fled Vietnam by boat to escape the war and the political troubles there. Many made their way to British Columbia, where they were welcomed with generosity. Groups of residents got together to help the newcomers adjust to their new life.

The Doukhobors

Many newcomers had difficulty adjusting to life in British Columbia. The Doukhobors (DUKE-uh-bors) were a group of newcomers from Russia who practised their own religion. Among their ideas was a strong belief in non-violence. When the Russian government forced the Doukhobors to fight in the army, many of them left their homeland for Canada, where they were promised they could live in peace.

In 1908, a group of several thousand Doukhobors settled in eastern British Columbia. They lived together in large houses and operated farms and businesses. For the most part they avoided contact with other people. They preferred to follow their religion and educate their children themselves.

As time went on, the government began to force Doukhobor children to attend public schools. Some parents resisted, and a long period of unrest began. Schools were burned, protest marches were held and many Doukhobors were arrested. They wanted to be left alone to follow their own lifestyle. The government felt that the Doukhobors had to conform to the rules like everyone else.

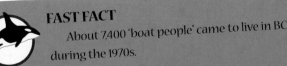

FAST FACT
About 7,400 "boat people" came to live in BC during the 1970s.

BC People
KEEPING THE WORLD GREEN

The organization Greenpeace has a huge army of activists fighting to stop pollution and protect wildlife around the world. But in 1970, Greenpeace was a small group of people in Vancouver who wanted to put a stop to the testing of nuclear bombs by the United States in the ocean near Alaska. These protestors hired an old skipper and his rundown fish boat, the *Phyllis Cormack*, and sailed north toward the test site. Their plan was to put themselves in the middle of the test site and dare the American government to blow them up.

As it turned out, the boat was stopped by bad weather, and the bomb test went ahead. But the protest got so much support that the Americans agreed to stop nuclear testing.

The new organization called itself Greenpeace and started a new campaign, to stop the killing of whales. They tracked down the whaling ships far out at sea and tried to shield the whales from the hunters. Once again Greenpeace attracted a lot of attention, this time to the slaughter of the whales. Due in part to their efforts, the whale hunt ceased.

Today Greenpeace has headquarters in Europe and followers around the world. Not everyone approves of the tactics it uses, but Greenpeace has been very successful in drawing public attention to the destruction of the environment.

The crew of the Phyllis Cormack *on a voyage to protest nuclear testing, 1971. Robert Keziere photo*

Greenpeace members erect a wind farm on the lawn of the BC Legislature to bring attention to renewable forms of energy, May 2004. *Greenpeace*

Finally, in the 1960s, the protests petered out. Younger Doukhobors adjusted to life in the wider society and other British Columbians grew to accept their different culture. Some Doukhobors still live in Grand Forks, Castlegar and other Interior towns. Many still speak Russian, practise their religion and work to keep their traditions alive.

Aboriginal People

In the years following World War II, Aboriginal people came to be more accepted by non-Aboriginal people in British Columbia. Many First Nations people had fought for Canada in the war as soldiers and it seemed unfair to deny them equal rights. In 1951, the

Rosemary Brown was a social worker in Vancouver when she won election to the legislature for the NDP in 1972. She was the first Black woman ever elected to political office anywhere in Canada. She worked in politics for fourteen years before retiring.

BC Archives I-32427

ban on the potlatch was ended. First Nations could now practise their own ceremonies without fear of going to jail. In 1960, First Nations people were given the right to vote in elections.

Another change that took longer to bring about was the closing of the residential schools. These schools had been in operation for decades. Government officials took First Nations children from their families and sent them to live at the schools. They were not allowed to speak their own languages and they were taught that their own cultures were inferior. The purpose of the schools was to force Aboriginal people to become part of the mainstream society.

Some residential schools turned out to be terrible places. Disease was common, and many youngsters died. Some of the teachers were cruel and mistreated the children.

In the 1960s the government began to close the residential schools. The last one closed in BC in the mid-1980s. The government recognized that it was wrong to try to destroy First Nations culture.

Bennett Too

No government lasts forever. After twenty years in office, W.A.C. Bennett lost the support of the voters in the 1972 election. Some people felt that he was using up the resources of the province just to remain in power. Others felt it was time to give someone else a chance at running the government.

In Their Own Words
SHIRLEY STERLING

Shirley Sterling, a First Nations writer and teacher, wrote a book about her experiences at residential school.

At school we get up at six o'clock every morning. As soon as sister rings the bell, we kneel on the floor and say our prayers. Then we get up and take turns washing and brushing our teeth. We're not allowed to talk…

After Mass we put on our smocks over our uniforms and line up for breakfast… We get gooey mush with powder milk and brown sugar. We say grace before and after every meal.

After breakfast we have jobs to do like clean the bathrooms or dust the halls and sweep stairs. After our jobs are finished we put our smocks in our closets and line up to go to class…

Supper is usually cabbage stew, two slices of bread with margarine, and wrinkled apples for dessert. Friday night is my favourite because we get oatmeal cookies for dessert.

From *My Name is Seepeetza*, Shirley Sterling (Toronto: Groundwood, 1992).

BC People
TOTEM POLE CARVERS

In the 1950s and 1960s, the arts of the Aboriginal people, which had been suppressed for many years, began to revive. This was especially true of totem poles, the tall wooden monuments that stood in front of houses, graveyards and villages along the coast.

In 1952, the Royal BC Museum in Victoria hired Mungo Martin, a skilled carver, to restore some of the museum's poles. Martin belonged to the Kwakwaka'wakw (kwalk-WAH-kah-walk) people. The poles he made were put up in Thunderbird Park at the museum, where they can be visited today. Martin also built a traditional longhouse at the site.

Mungo Martin trained many younger carvers to follow in his footsteps. Aboriginal carvers have made some of the finest works of art produced in British Columbia.

Mungo Martin, a renowned Aboriginal carver, at work on a pole in the carving shed at Thunderbird Park, at the Royal BC Museum in Victoria, 1961. BC Archives I-26829

Aboriginal students at a residential school at Alberni on Vancouver Island in the 1930s. BC Archives B-01060

Bennett retired from politics after his defeat. But the Social Credit Party remained in the family. His son Bill became leader and, in 1975, led the party to an election victory. Bill became premier like his father, and Social Credit formed the government for another sixteen years.

Expo 86

In the summer of 1986, Vancouver turned one hundred years old. The city celebrated by welcoming the world to a huge party, called Expo 86. It was the first international fair ever held in British Columbia.

Expo 86 took place along the waterfront of False Creek in the middle of downtown. False Creek had once been the site of sawmills, lumberyards and factories. It was made over for the fair to become a bustling centre of pavilions, restaurants, plazas and thrill rides. In the city's poorer neighbourhoods, tenants were evicted from their apartments so that the owners could rent them to visitors.

Some people argued that Expo 86 was a waste of money that should have been spent on education, health care and programs for the needy. Others argued that the fair brought a surge of tourist dollars to the province. After the fair was over and the visitors went home, Vancouver was left with a new transit system and many new buildings that had been constructed for Expo. The site of the fair was sold and the fairground was replaced by high-rise condominiums and other developments.

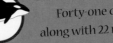

FAST FACT
Forty-one countries took part in Expo 86, along with 22 million visitors.

The fair seemed to express a new confidence in the city, and the province. British Columbians were happy to be the centre of the world's attention. They were proud to show off what the years of prosperity had accomplished.

Canada Place is a large conference centre and hotel on the Vancouver waterfront. It was built for Expo 86 and has become known to locals as "the building with the sails." It is also a terminal for cruise ships that carry passengers north up the coast to Alaska.

The Chinese Gate in Victoria, constructed in 1981.

MODERN TIMES

Histroy is the study of the past. It tells us how people used to live in times before our own. History also tells us about the present. It tells us how the world we live in came to be the way it is. Not only that, history can prepare us for the future. By helping us to understand how things changed in the past, it helps get us ready to deal with changes yet to come. Change brings new challenges. As the world becomes different, we have to adapt to new situations.

A Long, Hot Summer

Clayoquot Sound is a wilderness area of islands, beach and forest on the west coast of Vancouver Island. It lies in the territory of the Nuu-chah-nulth people. The unspoiled beauty of this area attracts whale watchers, hikers, kayakers and other outdoor adventurers.

In the summer of 1993, another type of visitor arrived in Clayoquot—protestors who were angry that loggers were allowed to cut trees in the river valleys running into the sound. The protestors set up blockades across the dirt roads and would not let the logging trucks pass.

Loggers asked the courts to open the roads so they could do their work. Police arrested more than nine hundred protesters during the summer. It was the largest number of people

Protesters at Clayoquot Sound in 1993. Collection of Ruth Masters

A kermode bear in BC's coastal rainforest. This is the only place in the world where these beautiful white creatures live. It has been illegal to hunt a kermode since 1965, and in 2001 the provincial government created a special sanctuary on the coast to protect them. Ian MacAllister photo

arrested at one time in Canadian history. Some had to pay fines; others had to serve time in prison. As a result of the summer of protest, the government made stricter rules for logging companies in Clayoquot. As well, some of the companies promised to make changes so that logging would be less damaging to the landscape.

Saving BC's Natural Resources

The Clayoquot protest was one of many taking place in the forests of British Columbia during the 1990s. For years logging had been a mainstay of the province's economy, producing jobs and income for many people. But as more and more of the forest disappeared, people began to worry that soon it would all be gone. What would be left for their children and grandchildren to enjoy?

Clear-cut logging in the Clayoquot region. Jacqueline Windh photo

Protests also stopped a copper mine near the Tatshenshini (*TAT-shen-SHEE-nee*) River in the far north of the province. The "Tat" is one of the best places in the world for seeing grizzly bears and other wild animals. Scientists warned that the mine might destroy the habitat where the bears lived. In response, the provincial government created a provincial park to protect some of the watershed.

Meanwhile, wild salmon also seemed to be in danger of disappearing. For decades the BC fishing fleet had harvested these valuable fish as they made their way back to the rivers and streams to spawn. But during the 1990s the numbers of salmon dropped. The government stepped in to set a limit on the number fishers were allowed to catch. Many people predicted that salmon fishing would have to stop completely to allow the fish time to recover.

British Columbians have always relied on their natural resources to produce wealth. But these resources do not last forever, and the quest for wealth may eventually use them up if they are not preserved.

In the 1990s, more and more people began talking about *sustainable development*. This means that instead of wiping out all the resources, we must replace them at the same rate at which we are using them. In this way, we leave something for future generations to enjoy. And if certain resources cannot be replaced, then we must find ways to preserve them.

The challenge faced by British Columbians is to maintain a decent level of wealth without destroying the natural resources that were once so plentiful.

Fish farms, such as this one off the Broughton Archipelago, have sparked much opposition. Greenpeace

will spread from the farmed fish to wild fish, and that sewage from the farms will pollute coastal waters. They also worry about the impact of fish farming on the livelihood of people who catch wild fish for a living.

Fish farming is a young industry and no one knows for sure what long-term impact it will have on the ocean. Meanwhile, farms raise thousands of tonnes of salmon each year, which is sold in markets and stores alongside fish caught in the wild.

Making Treaties with the First Nations

When Europeans first arrived in British Columbia, they found many different First Nations groups living here. Gradually the newcomers took over the land, forcing the First Nations to live apart on small plots of land called reserves.

In the Prairie provinces and in most of eastern Canada, the First Nations signed treaties with the government. They gave up their land in return for reserves, money and other benefits. In British Columbia, however, only a very few First Nations made treaties with the government. The rest have no treaties or other agreements.

The government argued that First Nations in British Columbia had no rights to their lands. On their side, First Nations argued that they had never given up their territories. The courts ruled several times in favour of the First Nations. As a result, in 1993, the BC government agreed to discuss treaties. It set up a BC Treaty

Farming Fish

Since the 1980s, fish farms—mainly salmon farms—have opened in sheltered waters along the coast of British Columbia. The farms are floating cages inside which salmon are raised until they are large enough to sell to stores and restaurants.

Supporters of salmon farming say that it is better to grow our own fish than to use up stocks of wild salmon. They compare fish farming to raising chickens or beef cattle and say that it is just as safe.

Critics of fish farming worry that diseases

BC People
RUNNING FOR HOPE

When Terry Fox lost a leg to bone cancer, he did not give up. Instead he decided to do something to fight the disease. In April 1980, when he was twenty-one years old, he began to run across Canada to raise money for cancer research. Fox started in St. John's, Newfoundland, and ran 5,373 kilometres to Sudbury, Ontario. His "Marathon of Hope" ended when the disease forced him to stop, but not before he raised millions of dollars for his cause.

Terry Fox died in 1981. Every year the run held in his memory in communities across Canada and in countries around the world brings in more money for medical research. In Vancouver, a statue of the young runner stands outside BC Place Stadium.

Gail Harvey/Terry Fox Foundation

BC People
THE NISGA'A

The Nisga'a people live in the valley of the Nass River in northern British Columbia. They consider this territory to be their homeland. For one hundred years they refused to give up this claim.

In 1973, the Supreme Court of Canada made a ruling in favour of the Nisga'a. Because of the court, the federal government agreed to begin negotiations. The BC provincial government also agreed to take part, and the result was a historic agreement signed in 1998.

The Nisga'a agreement gave the Nisga'a people $190 million, more than 2,000 square kilometres of land in the Nass Valley, a share of the salmon from the river and other benefits. Many other First Nations are negotiating with the government to have their own agreements for their own territories.

Commission to supervise the discussions.

It will take many years to make agreements with the First Nations. People on both sides hope that the treaty-making process will result in better relations between First Nations and other residents of British Columbia.

A Multicultural Society

During the 1990s, the population of British Columbia grew faster than that of any other province in Canada. Most of the growth was the result of immigration, the arrival of newcomers from other places. Immigrants had been coming to British Columbia ever since the first explorers landed. The difference was that in the 1990s, most of the newcomers came from countries in Asia.

By the end of the 1990s, about 20 percent of British Columbians, or one in five, had come from Hong Kong, China, India, Japan and other Asian countries. Most of the newcomers lived in Vancouver and the surrounding area. By 2001, there were as many British Columbians

In Their Own Words
JOSEPH GOSNELL

Joseph Gosnell was a chief of the Nisga'a people. In 1998 he came to Victoria to give a speech about the Nisga'a Treaty in the legislature. He called the treaty a "triumph for all British Columbians."

A triumph, I believe, which proves to the world that reasonable people can sit down and settle historical wrongs. It proves that a modern society can correct the mistakes of the past. A triumph because, under the treaty the Nisga'a people will join Canada and British Columbia as free citizens—full and equal participants in the social, economic and political life of this province, of this country. A triumph because under the treaty we will no longer be wards of the state, no longer beggars in our own lands.

Gary Fiegehen photo

FAST FACT
About 2,500 Nisga'a people live in communities along the Nass River.

for whom English was a second language as there were people who spoke English at home. In some neighbourhoods, as many as eighty different languages were spoken.

This is news because British Columbia had generally considered itself a "British" province, as its name suggests. For a long time most of the people living here came from Great Britain, the United States or eastern Canada. They had always thought of themselves as the majority. Now statistics were showing that British

In the middle of bustling downtown Vancouver there is a place of peace and tranquility. It is the Dr. Sun Yat-Sen Classical Chinese Garden, opened in 1986. This is the first garden of its kind outside China. All the materials used to build it, from the roof tiles to the rocks on the ground, were imported from China. Dr. Sun Yat-Sen Classical Chinese Garden

Columbia was a very multicultural province.

Of course, British Columbia has always been a mix of people from different backgrounds. Chinese miners and railway workers, Japanese farmers and fishers, millworkers from India, Black homesteaders, Doukhobor settlers from Russia—all these and many others have been part of the society. However, since the 1960s, many more people from Asia, Africa and the Caribbean came to live in BC. In the process they created an even more mixed society of people from many backgrounds.

A multicultural society is one in which people of many different backgrounds live together. The differences create variety and new ideas. Sometimes they also create misunderstanding and conflict, when people from different backgrounds with different beliefs find it difficult to get along with one another.

FAST FACT
After English, more people in BC speak Chinese than any other language.

The challenge for British Columbians is to create a society in which everyone feels welcome to participate, and no one is held back because of the colour of their skin, their religious beliefs or the country that they or their ancestors come from.

A New Economy

The economy of British Columbia has changed dramatically during the past decades. The economy used to rely on its natural products—timber, minerals and fish. These are still very important, but much less so than they once were.

Today, many more jobs are in the *knowledge industries*—making and sharing information. Examples are computer programmers, medical researchers and engineers. These people do not catch fish, cut down trees or dig up minerals. Instead, they work with information to produce new products.

Another growing area is the *service industries*. Workers in this sector provide services to other people, working as waiters, teachers, store clerks, bus drivers, people who furnish government services to residents and tourists, and many others.

Fewer and fewer people are working in the resource industries of BC. This is because the resources themselves are becoming more scarce. It is also because machines are doing much of the work once done by people. Mills need far fewer workers to produce lumber. As stocks of wild fish appear to decline, far fewer fishers are needed to bring in the catch. The

FAST FACT
Farming, fishing, logging and mining still produce about three-quarters of all the goods that BC sells to other places. But less than 10 percent of the workforce hold jobs in these industries.

Top Five Industries in British Columbia Ranked by the Number of Workers

1. **retail** (salespeople in stores)
2. **health care and social assistance** (doctors, nurses, hospital workers, social workers)
3. **manufacturing** (factory and millworkers)
4. **hospitality** (hotels and restaurants)
5. **education** (schoolteachers and university and college professors)

question is: will there be new jobs to replace the ones that are lost?

The challenge for British Columbians is to adjust to the new economy. New jobs have to be found for young people just starting out in the workforce. And many people who were fishers, loggers or miners will have to learn new skills to take up jobs in the new industries.

One resource industry that has boomed in recent years is the oil and natural gas industry. It is centred in the northeast corner of the province around Fort St. John. Oil and gas lie in vast pools beneath the earth's surface. Once wells are dug, the resource is pumped to the surface, then carried to the southern parts of BC through long pipelines.

Large amounts of gas and oil are known to exist below the ocean floor off the north coast of BC as well. Some people believe BC should install platforms in the ocean to drill for this resource. The province of Newfoundland has been producing oil and gas this way for years. Other people worry about the dangers of oil leaking into the water and onto the beaches, killing wildlife and fouling the environment. This issue remains very controversial.

Livable Cities

Another challenge facing British Columbia is to keep the cities livable. Three-quarters of the population of the province lives in Greater Vancouver—a huge, sprawling mass of highways and high-rise buildings—and more people move to the area every year. All of them need somewhere to live. They need more roads to drive on, more parks to relax in, more buses to take to work and more dumps to take care of all the garbage.

Every *hour* two new cars join the traffic that already crowds Vancouver's streets. This makes it harder to move around the city. It also means that the air is getting dirtier and harder to breathe.

Air pollution is just one of the problems caused by rapid growth. Another is the disappearance of green spaces—park and farmland that is gobbled up to build houses for the newcomers. Yet another problem is the chemical waste and other pollutants of a growing city, which threaten the supply of clean drinking water.

The challenge for British Columbians is to make room for all the newcomers, while at the same time keeping our cities clean, safe places to live.

The Olympic Games

On July 3, 2003, British Columbia held its breath and waited. Finally the envelope was opened and the announcement was made. The

FAST FACT
Every year, 50,000 more people come to live in Vancouver.

Vancouver is a high density city.

The resort of Whistler, where the Olympic skiing events will take place in 2010, is 120 kilometres from Vancouver. It opened in 1980 and has grown to become one of the top mountain resorts in the world.

2010 Winter Olympic Games would be taking place in Vancouver and the nearby mountain resort of Whistler.

The announcement ended five years of planning and debate. It takes a lot of preparation to host the Olympics. Sports arenas and ski hills must be built, along with housing for all the athletes who will arrive from all over the world for the sixteen-day event. Highways, transit systems and airports need to be improved to accommodate all the visitors. What's more, Vancouver and Whistler will also host the Paralympic Winter Games for athletes with disabilities.

Not everyone wanted BC to host the Olympics. It will cost billions of dollars to pay for the Games, much of which will come from BC taxpayers. Some people argued that the money should be spent on other, more important things. Olympic supporters argued that in the end, the benefits will outweigh the costs.

Soon after the announcement in 2003, British Columbians were hard at work getting ready to host the 2010 Olympics. The challenge is to have everything ready on time, and to put on a good show for all the people around the world who will be watching on television.

A History of Challenges

As British Columbians begin a new century, they face important challenges.

Some of these challenges are:

• saving the natural environment from being spoiled,

• making fair agreements with the First Nations people,

• learning to live with people of different backgrounds and beliefs,

• making the cities safe, clean places to live,

• training for jobs in a new economy.

History shows us that British Columbia

has always been a place where people had challenges to face. The story of the province is the story of how these challenges were met and solved.

History gives us confidence that we can meet the challenges of the present, just as our parents and their parents before them met the challenges of the past.

Timeline

TIMELINE

8500 BCE	The first inhabitants of British Columbia are living in the Peace River country in the north.
1778	Captain James Cook and his crew arrive in two ships on the west coast of Vancouver Island.
1785	The first ship arrives on the coast of British Columbia to trade for sea-otter skins.
1792–94	Captain George Vancouver explores the coast.
1793	Alexander Mackenzie arrives at the Pacific Ocean after crossing North America on foot and by canoe.
1805	Fur traders build the first trading post in British Columbia.
1808	Simon Fraser canoes to the mouth of the Fraser River.
1827	Fort Langley is built on the Fraser River.
1843	Fort Victoria, the headquarters of the fur trade in British Columbia, opens.
1849	The colony of Vancouver Island is created.
1850	For the first time, gold is discovered in BC by outsiders when the Haida on the Queen Charlotte Islands trade some gold nuggets with the Hudson's Bay Company.
1856	Aboriginal people show gold nuggets to the trader at Fort Kamloops.

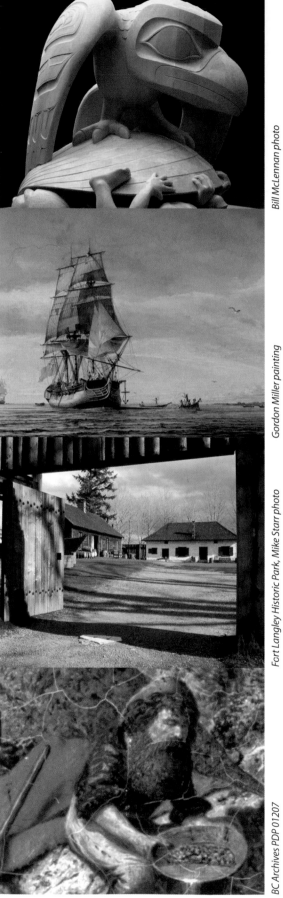

Bill McLennan photo

Gordon Miller painting

Fort Langley Historic Park, Mike Starr photo

BC Archives PDP 01207

1858	The first shipload of prospectors arrives in Victoria from San Francisco.
1858	The mainland of British Columbia becomes a separate colony.
1859	The townsite of New Westminster, capital of the new colony, is laid out by military surveyors.
1862	The town of Barkerville is founded in the Cariboo.
1862	A smallpox epidemic devastates the Aboriginal population.
1865	The Cariboo Road reaches Barkerville.
1866	The colony on the mainland joins with Vancouver Island to become a single colony called British Columbia.
1868	The high point of the Cariboo gold rush has passed.
1871	The colony of British Columbia becomes a province of Canada.
1871	The first successful salmon cannery opens near the mouth of the Fraser River.
1880	Construction begins on the British Columbia section of the Canadian Pacific Railway.
1885	The Last Spike ceremony occurs at Craigellachie, completing the railway across the continent
1885	The government bans the potlatch ceremony.

Vancouver Public Library, 23430

BC Archives A-00350

BC Archives A-00613

Canadian Pacific Railway Archives A.1340

1886	The first train arrives in Vancouver after crossing the continent from Montreal.
1886	The City of Vancouver is created.
1890	The first electric streetcars begin operation in Victoria.
1896	The smelter at Trail begins operation, treating ore from the mines at nearby Rossland. It grows to become the largest smelter in the world.
1898	A great fire destroys much of New Westminster.
1906	The Grand Trunk Pacific Railway begins clearing a site for the city of Prince Rupert.
1907	Rioters destroy property in Vancouver's Chinatown.
1912	Miners go on strike in Nanaimo coal mines; the strike lasts two years.
1913	Railway construction through Hells Gate causes landslides that almost wipe out the Fraser River salmon run.
1914–18	World War I rages in Europe.
1929	The stock market crash begins the Great Depression.
1932	The BC government begins setting up relief camps for single men without work.
1935	Unemployed protestors in BC begin the On-to-Ottawa Trek.

BC Archives D-08738

BC Archives B-08416

BC Archives B-00312

City of Vancouver Archives Re N8.2

1938	Protest by unemployed people results in bloody violence in Vancouver streets.
1939	World War II begins.
1942	The government forces Japanese Canadians to leave their homes on the coast.
1945	World War II ends.
1951	The ban on the potlatch is withdrawn.
1952	The Social Credit Party wins its first election and W.A.C. Bennett becomes premier.
1958	British Columbia celebrates its 100th birthday.
1965	Simon Fraser University opens on a mountaintop in Burnaby.
1972	After twenty years as premier, W.A.C. Bennett loses an election to the NDP.
1986	Expo 86 attracts visitors from around the world to Vancouver.
1993	The summer of protest at Clayoquot Sound on Vancouver Island.
1998	Signing of the Nisga'a Agreement.
2003	Vancouver and Whistler win the competition to host the 2010 Winter Olympic Games and Paralympic Games.

Claude P. Dettloff photo, National Archives C38723

BC Ferries